HEAD IN THE SAND,
DEATH IN THE CLOUDS

Head in the Sand, Death in the Clouds

John A. Shewmaker DO

CONTENTS

1

DEATH IN A CLOUD

THE ORIGINAL AIM of this book was to explore medically related fatal crashes in various aviation platforms. This is important for several reasons. Specifically, I want to help people understand that some airframes have very safe records when operated by safe individuals and that they have very unsafe records when operated by unsafe individuals. It reminds me of the "Guns don't kill; people kill" slogan.

Over the course of writing a previous book, *Murder in a 172*, and while planning this book, the concept and message morphed into a diatribe and indictment of a process or, to be more accurate, the exposure of the lack of a process.

The goal has now become to explore how the National Transportation Safety Board (NTSB) presents its accident investigations, to suggest simple and quite affordable changes to the system, and to look toward a future wherein the NTSB actually attempts to fully investigate general aviation accidents. Coupled with a few simple changes in protocol, we could then imagine a time in the near future when accident investigation does a service rather than a disservice to the aviation community and the public.

I'd like to be direct and brutal and not let those last sentences ebb. The current methodology the NTSB uses to present fatal general aviation accidents to the public is flawed, the information is incorrect, the actual investigation process shows a casual if not blatant disregard for reality, and the focus of the entire process appears to miss the obvious while focusing on the easy. Occasionally, the use of words by the investigators in specific accidents even suggests that some accident causes are intentionally not being reported. That would be a federal crime if it were the case.

It is easy to tear down an engine if you really enjoy tearing down engines. But if engines are not causing the vast majority of fatal accidents, maybe we should be focusing on what *is causing most accidents.* In other words, if 95 percent of fatal accidents are the result of human factors, why then isn't 95 percent of the NTSB's investigation focused upon the medical, mental, and physical attributes of the human who was flying the airplane when the crash occurred? The NTSB needs to grow up and start handling general aviation fatal accidents as if they are serious events instead of a chance to playact at being an accident investigator who thinks mechanical things are cool. The job entails finding truth. Pretending you tried and then overtly demonstrating you didn't is the antithesis of finding truth.

I think that was harsh enough. Honest and brutally so. And it needs to be said, repeated, and—perhaps by the victims' families—screamed.

The first platform we investigate is the Cirrus group of airplanes. These have been the best-selling single-engine, four-seat airplanes for the past eleven years. There are more than six thousand of them in service as of June 2015, according to the Cirrus Corporation. They additionally have a whole-plane parachute system for added safety.

If most of this airplane's fatal accidents were caused by medical reasons, then, for the healthy and competent pilot, it should be considered a safe platform and worthy of the adulation many of its owners give it. After all, the overall fatal-accident rate is only about 1 percent, far lower than the simpler Cessna 172 airframe I explored in *Murder in a 172.* The airplane isn't the problem; the sub-segment of pilots who have no regard for their own health is the issue.

The Cirrus is not a model for people who live on a shoestring, however. The airframe is an expensive, top-of-the-line single-engine airplane. A person who purchases such a vehicle is investing a lot of money. But does this equate to a person also investing his or her time wisely into safety?

There have been seventy-five fatal Cirrus accidents since 1996 for which the NTSB has published a report.

These reports can be accessed at NTSB.gov by looking at both the accident dockets and the aviation database. My suggestion is to read the narrative reports first and then the probable-cause reports. The docket can then be used to confirm the information. As you will soon see, it can also give us some added clues as to the thoroughness of the NTSB's investigative effort.

The first two fatal Cirrus accidents are excluded here, as the airplane was undergoing flight testing at the time. They were not part of the merchandised items sold to the flying public. Because test flights, by their very nature, invoke a risk I'm not attempting to assess, this seems a reasonable approach. Thus we are left with seventy-three incidents to explore.

2

LULLING YOU TO SLEEP

LAX01FA145

IN THE FIRST fatal accident, in which three people were killed, the airplane was flown into clouds by the non-instrument-flight-rules-rated (non-IFR) pilot and after entering clouds, the airplane struck a mountain.

The weather reports for the day in question weren't great, but given that there were no other significant medical findings and that there was no attempt to look at the past decisions the pilot had made, I lean toward calling this an example of bad judgment versus pathologically bad judgment. But after rereading the probable-cause report, should I reconsider?

> The composite aircraft impacted the side of a mountain approximately 20 minutes prior to sunset after the non-instrument-rated private pilot departed on a cross-country flight. The pilot obtained printed weather information via a DUATs system approximately 9 hours prior to the flight's departure. AIRMETS for mountain obscurement, moderate turbulence, and moderate rime/mixed icing conditions were in effect, and included the area of the accident site.

Previous weather observations from the departure airport reported snow showers located over the mountains in the vicinity of the flight's route. A witness located near the accident site, reported he could not see the base of the mountain throughout the day due to sleet, snow, rain, and wind. Nearby airport weather observations indicated VFR weather conditions; however, forecasts for the flight route indicated there was still a chance of mountain obscurement. No evidence was found that the pilot obtained updated weather information for the route of flight prior to taking off. No anomalies were noted that would have prevented normal aircraft operation.

Here I'd like to make a point.

All people make bad decisions and choices and have bad days. However, if there is no real way to assess their overall mind-sets and decision-making capabilities, it is safest to err on the side of the pilots and not demean them or their memories. That would be a disservice to aviation safety as well. This accident, with only this information, no medical history, and a negative toxicology report—what do we call it? Or can we? Is the investigation truly complete? We have no idea of the pilot's mental and medical history. It is as obscure as the mountain peak into which he crashed. And what about the two passengers? Has the investigation done justice to their memories?

The bodies were found four days after the crash. Is toxicology of any value four days later? Furthermore, is a negative toxicology report going to be where you decide to stop investigating a crash that involved two innocent victims? Or, is a toxicology report simply one piece of evidence you gather before you begin a thorough assessment of a pilot's past health and habits? These questions are addressed and finally answered as we move through the book.

For all we know, the pilot's health-insurance records showed he was a completely healthy person. On the other hand, for all we know, he had a history of mental illness and frequently stopped his medication.

What does a person with mental illness have in his toxicology report if he stops his medication? Accident investigations done properly would gather obvious basic information such as a pilot's medical records and health-insurance records. This should be obvious even to a child. These records are amazingly simple to get, and it costs nothing if done properly. This accident wasn't fully investigated. Two innocent passengers died, and an investigation was concluded prior to ever even beginning.

NYC02FA089

The second fatal accident occurred when two pilots lost control of their aircraft and entered a spin. For unknown reasons, they didn't deploy the plane's ballistic parachute and perished. They had bought the airplane six days prior. The toxicology reports again appear to have been all the medical information deemed worthy of inspection if the accident docket and narrative reports are complete. But again, does a negative toxicology report tell us anything of value? It sounds good, but is it of any true significance in an accident investigation? For example, what if one of the pilots had Alzheimer's disease? Apparently it wasn't investigated.

FTW02FA162

In the next report, high-density altitude and a mountain came together, causing the death of the sole occupant. Witnesses described to the letter what happens at a high-density altitude to an aircraft attempting to climb above its adjusted service ceiling. The NTSB investigation tore into the aircraft parts aggressively, all the while certainly realizing this was pretty obviously a density-altitude issue. To the investigators' credit, they must rule out the relatively rare instance of mechanical failure. To their shame, they did no such justice to past medical issues, which are exponentially more important in most fatal crashes.

The toxicology report was negative. Case closed, move on, nothing to see here.

In mechanical terms, this would be like saying, "We found the fuel tank; therefore, there was no mechanical issue with this crash." As absolutely bizarre as that may sound to you now, by the time we are done here, you will realize the truth of this paragraph. A negative toxicology report is no different at all from finding the plane's battery in working condition. It says absolutely nothing about what caused the accident. A negative toxicology report certainly in no way excludes a medical cause of the accident. This accident investigation was closed prior to being fully investigated.

FTW03FA029

Next we have a combination of events, all leading to what is obviously a medically related accident. The bottom line is that if you are going to take a highly sedating medication (Benadryl), it is not a great idea to take your six-figure toy out for a joy flight across twelve hundred miles of the United States. And it is especially important that you not fly into icing or IMC (instrument meteorological conditions), particularly if you are only a VFR (visual flight rules) pilot. The choices this pilot made were choices a rational person would never make.

This gentleman, who was not IFR rated, didn't bother to check weather in the area he was about to fly into after landing for a refueling stop. He flew low and slow into heavy fog. The presence of Benadryl in his system suggests allergies, infection, or a sleep disorder. If the NTSB wished to look deeper into why the pilot felt he needed to take benadryl there is no evidentiary trail to suggest the NTSB followed through.

I would pose a question: Was the Benadryl an issue, or were the pilot's baseline judgment and choices the main issue? In an investigation with human error as a causative, it behooves us to assess the human's baseline of behavior. Let us also remember that when the accident occurred, he had been on the Benadryl for some time (presuming he took it prior to takeoff). Thus, three to four hours prior to the accident, during the planning stage of the trip and prior to departure, the impact of the medication within his bloodstream, acting on his brain and causing sedation and fatigue, would have been at a higher level. Part of any investigation should include finding out why he decided he needed Benadryl. People don't take medications out of a sadistic urge to confuse naive investigators looking at their corpses. They take medications because they have symptoms. In the case of Benadryl, insomnia or allergies are the usual culprits.

CHI03FA057

In the next accident, a pilot trying his best to avoid entering IMC (instrument meteorological conditions) ended up impacting terrain after attempting to fly about one hundred feet off the ground to avoid the scud layer. The weather at the beginning of the flight was marginal, and he was on decongestants. A passenger died, and the non-IFR-rated pilot did as well. I would call this a medically related crash, but I do understand the argument against that. The pilot knew the weather was marginal, and he was taking medication for some condition that perhaps made him marginal too. Endangering your passenger when you aren't IFR qualified by taking him or her into marginal VFR on a day when you aren't 100 percent is bad judgment that, to my mind, rises to the level of a medically significant issue.

LAX03FA072

This accident occurred during cross-country IFR daytime conditions, and the airplane was piloted by a gentleman astute enough not to fly a high-performance aircraft cross-country without first being IFR qualified. While he had dextromethorphan and pseudoephedrine in his system, indicating an underlying issue, he seemed far more on course than the controllers, who, through several missteps, guided him into terrain.

ATL04FA096

Medicine and judgment both played key roles in this accident.

The pilot was taking decongestants and a sedating antihistamine, had the aircraft at max weight, did not do any preflight engine run-up, and departed with the flaps improperly configured. His actions killed three other people. Arrogance, ignoring safety, ignoring preflight checklists, and taking medications that affect judgment resulted in committing homicide in the process. A real accident investigation that thoroughly investigated his past patterns of behavior was studiously avoided.

CHI04FA255

There was no clear medical issue that caused this flight to crash. The pilot died, and the passenger, a CFI (certified flight instructor), survived but stated he had no memory of the events leading to the stall and crash.

SEA05FA023

This was another crash into mountainous terrain, and it resulted in three deaths. The crash occurred when a pilot with three passengers decided to *buzz a glider twice* and then wasn't able to salvage the airplane as it turned down into a canyon. Only one of his passengers survived the aerial game of chicken. This was bad judgment, but because it was a singular event, I'd be hesitant to call it pathologically bad judgment, since there is no evidence of a more chronic behavioral pattern. When contrasted with the last two accidents cited, you can see where people could often disagree on the extent to which the accident was related to a medical or judgment issue. I try to err on the side of the pilot, since we are all human, and it serves no purpose to blindly assign a medical reason without a clear pattern of behavior justifying the argument. We need to look at a pilot's historical choices of behavior before deeming a singular event as a pathologically bad judgment. We all do stupid things in life; this is far different than living a life predominated by poor judgment.

To be clear—a singular event with no evidence of a pattern of bad judgments, I try to assign this a "nonmedical" or "unclear" rating. However, if there is evidence the pilot routinely made bad judgments, then I would argue that his or her final fatal bad judgment was part of a bigger medical or mental issue that was made predictable by the pilot's past behavior.

Having said all that, I can't foresee a case where I would endanger three passengers' lives for the thrill of buzzing a glider. We all have our differences. I'd also remind you that without any attempt at investigating what this pilot's previous life choices had entailed, we have almost no data with which to assess human factors. He was in an expensive airplane with three passengers, buzzing a glider. Twice. An investigator had a pretty good indication from the beginning that perhaps a deeper look was needed. But was the investigator even curious?

IAD05FA032

In this flight, the pilot became spatially disoriented during an IFR flight plan. There is nothing to suggest further medical issues.

SEA05FA038

In this particular crash, the one detail that tips the scale for me is that the pilot *was* advised not to attempt a night VFR flight into an area of worsening weather, but he did so anyway. The saddest part of this crash is that he was IFR qualified, filed an IFR plan, knew the weather, checked it several times, and then canceled the IFR plan and flew VFR. This was a very bad decision that may have cost him and two others their lives. In the final analysis, not knowing the situation, I tip ever so slightly to a medical/judgment issue, but it wouldn't take much to push me in the other direction. I say this because this was a business flight, and he was flying his employer, and I have no real feel for the owner-pilot relationship. The added pressures of a nonpilot employer pressuring a pilot to fly beyond his capabilities isn't a new phenomenon, and the resulting cemetery isn't a small place.

The fact that he had a history of "scud running" under low ceilings, per the report, is what really makes this a tough call. A pattern of bad judgment is more of a pathology issue than a momentary judgment lapse brought on by the external pressures one might expect in an employee-employer relationship at the end of a business trip.

It is accidents such as the last four that inspired me to write this book—these borderline calls that make each of us look in the mirror and ask, "Would I fly that day? Am I qualified to speak to another's ability?" It is humbling, and it isn't a route to take with a casual eye. In fact, that is the whole point. You either investigate fully or you do a disservice to all parties. This book is wholly focused on the fact that this disservice is being perpetuated over and over in these investigations.

Thus far, we have seen bad judgment, arrogance, showboating, and inner-ear inputs (spatial disorientation) as the prime reasons behind most of the accidents. I have never seen a single toxicology report that identifies an arrogance level or an autopsy that identifies a level of showboating or judgment. The inner ear appears to be pretty much ignored by most forensic pathologists during autopsy.

LAX05FA088

This accident is an example of something we don't often see in the light-sport group. It illustrates a significant difference in training and ability, and it illustrates the dangers of higher-altitude and higher-performance airframes that are close to being "all-weather" aircraft. Occasionally these aircraft will encounter "all weather" and come up short of the definition.

In this solo fatality accident, the pilot received errant weather reports and inadvertently flew into icing conditions. He attempted to deploy the parachute; however, the airspeed limits of the system caused it to separate from the aircraft. There is no evidence of medical factors.

CHI06FA043

This was a crash that killed three. In this event, a pilot with two passengers obtained weather reports and was advised that VFR flight wasn't recommended, owing to IMC conditions. He took two others to their deaths anyway. While he was instrument rated, he had three total hours of actual instrument time and only one hour in the past ninety days. Given the situation, the fact that he proceeded VFR after being warned, and that two passengers perished, I'll err on the side of the innocent victims and call it medical/judgment related.

To make the larger point: when an expert on weather advises you not to fly into that weather, you as the pilot have to process that information and make a go or no-go decision. Additionally, you have to process your own skill set, subjectively and based on your reading, lessons, and instructions, and objectively to a degree. Putting all this together and deciding *go* happens in one's brain. That is why this is a medical crash. A rational person doesn't listen to a weather expert tell her that VFR isn't recommended and ignore that fact, while also ignoring her training, reading, and knowledge of her own abilities.

ATL06FA029

The next flight again concerns bad judgment, a pilot flying into IMC conditions. Although he had an IFR rating, he hadn't logged any IFR hours in the past ninety days. He and his passenger perished. Again, given the weather briefing he received and his lack of real currency, I am pushed into calling this a medically related crash, but I'll admit you could argue it's a borderline call for now.

Would it take much insight into his personal life and habits to sway me or you to the other side? That is the reality of marginal accident reports. They don't paint the picture; they just use a bit of Jackson Pollock, a hint of Picasso, and then they critique by combining Lewis Carroll with some Gertrude Stein. Until we actually fully investigate an accident, we shouldn't expect to have much in the way of real answers.

LAX06FA087

In this flight, the pilot and his instructor were doing touch-and-goes, practicing emergency procedures. The actual emergency was the fact that the instructor had marijuana in his system and the pilot had antidepressants in his. This flight should never have happened, because the pilot legally couldn't be flying with antidepressants in his system; nor could the instructor legally be flying with evidence of marijuana usage. Two people died, but I am hard pressed to find a victim, except for those 80 to 90 percent of pilots who utilize good judgment and who are negatively impacted when criminal actions and bad judgment reflect poorly on aviation. Those who give aviation a bad name are, to my mind, the largest issue we face in aviation. These people give the nonflying public a bad impression of who is really out there flying. These criminals also are among the most vocal critics of the FAA. Criminals don't like a spotlight upon them when they lie to the FAA after landing on closed runways.

We have now looked at fifteen Cirrus accidents. These have been fairly bland. Eight of the fifteen were related to IFR or icing conditions. Sedating drugs were present in three accidents. Medical records? Hmm, pause a second and reflect. We haven't seen medical records, have we? That is because the pilots' medical records are not routinely assessed. That is going to become a bigger theme as we dig deeper. We also aren't seeing a lot of parachute deployment, despite several of the accidents being examples of a crash wherein the emergency procedures call for activation of the ballistic parachute device.

It is time to wake up, because the book is about to pick up speed. These first few accidents do hint at possible patterns:

1. Longer flights
2. Weather
3. Ice
4. Unpulled parachutes

These factors are not going to be helped by a pilot who isn't current in his training or who is drugged, medically impaired, or mentally impaired.

As we continue, these patterns become motifs of the higher-performance platform. Another motif is a lack of interest on the part of the NTSB in gaining any real understanding of the medical causes of airplane accidents. Up to now, that might not have seemed too interesting. Keep reading; that is about to change.

3

Hints of a Larger Problem

Prior to 2006, we saw that icing conditions as well as failure to pull the emergency parachute seemed to be critical issues in Cirrus fatalities. We also saw that of the first fifteen fatal accidents that had NTSB final narratives, three were certainly medical, and strong arguments could be made about the judgment exercised in many of the other accidents as well.

On February 4, 2006, another fatal Cirrus accident occurred.

MIA06FA050

Instrument conditions prevailed, and the pilot, his wife, and a passenger were all killed. The pilot and his wife were both IFR rated. No medical data were obtained other than their ages (sixty-seven and fifty-two, respectively) and a negative toxicology report. There is no evidence in the NTSB final narrative or probable-cause reports that any effort was made to obtain any medical records. The bodies were not recovered until a week after the accident and were submerged in salt water for this period of time. No discussion of the validity of toxicology testing on a submerged corpse and what that will or will not tell an examiner was mentioned. No commentary or suggestion was made that with a submerged corpse as the only source of information, perhaps a survey of past medical records would give some insight into the pilot's mental and physical health. If you have an accident investigation and you want to assess human factors, then actually attempting to investigate human factors is a good start.

Per the probable cause report:

The pilot took off in instrument meteorological flight conditions and, shortly thereafter, misinterpreted a series of air traffic control instructions to be for his airplane when they were for another airplane. Subsequent callouts and responses by the pilot indicated confusion, to the point where he stated, "I gotta get my act together here." Less than one minute later, the pilot reported "avionics problems," and about forty seconds after that, during his last transmission, he stated that he was "losin' it." The airplane subsequently descended nose-down, out of clouds, and impacted a house and terrain. The airplane was equipped with a primary flight display (PFD), as well as separate backup instruments in case the display failed. The airplane had approximately ninety-eight hours of operation since being manufactured, and it had a history of PFD failures. The pilot had previously practiced partial panel (no PFD) flight. The airplane was also equipped with a parachute system, which was not deployed in flight.

The National Transportation Safety Board determines the probable cause(s) of this accident as follows:

The pilot's failure to maintain aircraft control, which resulted in an uncontrolled descent to the ground. Factors included an avionics failure, pilot disorientation, and instrument meteorological conditions. A factor in the severity of the impact was the pilot's failure to deploy the airplane's onboard parachute system.

The question of previous PFD failures in a plane you paid a lot of money to buy and then flew to your death in IMC conditions seems to have not been worthy of NTSB discussion. It is a mind-set that makes me raise my eyebrows. The plane had a known history of display issues, and yet the pilot went into weather? Does this warrant a closer look at that pilot's mind and their medical history?

CHI06FA186

In this accident, which occurred in VFR conditions, the pilot expired in the hospital three weeks after the incident, and not one other single bit of medical information was placed in the final accident report—none. What we do know is that the pilot failed on the initial landing and attempted a go-around, which he was unable to execute. The probable-cause report lists an improper use of flaps. It doesn't report any medications or conditions that might have affected this sixty-six-year-old pilot's abilities to choose the flap setting.

There is nothing listed in the NTSB docket showing any attempt to gather medical records ever occurred. There is also no autopsy report listed. It is nonsensically easy for a government entity to obtain hospital records when a person is in the hospital and when the government entity has the legal right to do so. It involves filling out a one-page form and putting it in a fax machine, no, it is easier than that, fax machines have been computerized for 20 plus years. Evidently, no one bothered.

CHI06FA245

In August 2006 this accident killed the pilot and seriously injured three passengers. It occurred under IMC conditions.

The first thing that caught my eye was this comment in the NTSB report: "Although the accident pilot had recently undergone surgery, the CSIP pilot reported that the accident pilot was feeling good and that he had told the CSIP pilot that he did not feel any side effects and was not taking any medications."

Recent surgery? You would think the NTSB would clarify this. They don't; in fact, they seem to ignore it completely.

One interview stated, "Was he feeling OK? He was. He said he didn't feel any affects from the surgery. He said he was not on any medications. Feeling good and not taking medications."

Also reported in the docket were "medical stints." One would assume that this means *cardiac stents* (there are other types, far more benign).

One would also presume that proper poststenting procedure by any competent cardiologist would require follow-up and medications. I also presume that this is *not* the recent surgery the interviewee refers to. Recent cardiac stents would have made it illegal to fly, and the NTSB would surely have known this—one would hope. Thus, it appeared the recent surgery was something other than his coronary-artery disease.

I had to dig into a deposition with his wife to find out his true history. The pilot was an oral surgeon. He had had a hernia repair just four days prior to the flight.

1. He told his patients to avoid narcotics and use only ibuprofen or Tylenol.
2. He told his wife that was what he was going to do, because that was what he told his patients.
3. He was taking three blood pressure medications, antiplatelet medication, and aspirin.
4. He had had cardiac stents in three blood vessels.
5. He continued to have severe coronary-artery disease.
6. He had severe but treated sleep apnea that he may not have properly reported to the FAA.

These may or may not be pertinent. Does a person four days removed from hernia surgery recover sufficiently to make good decisions regarding flying airplanes? Does the fact that this person was an oral surgeon with a history of coronary-artery disease play any role?

Pain, ego, judgment, oxygenation status—these are issues that need to be fully discussed and not just in a witness interview, because we know that pain, ego, judgment, and oxygenation status can and have caused aviation accidents. Assessment of a fatal accident presumes a certain level of *thoroughness*.

Then, in the docket reports, I was able to find the following:

In 2003, the pilot had stenting of three heart vessels.

Also, regarding the hernia, the physician who performed the operation wrote him a prescription for a sedating narcotic. The operation was on August 24, 2006, four days prior to the accident; the surgeon felt the patient would need narcotics.

The autopsy showed that the pilot suffered from severe atherosclerotic heart disease.

The question now becomes, what was the pilot's ability to safely operate an aircraft?

1. He had severe atherosclerotic heart disease.
2. He had severe sleep apnea.
3. He had had surgery four days prior. He was given narcotics for pain by an expert who certainly knows they are addictive, knows they should be used sparingly, and felt the level of pain after the operation was such that, in his expert opinion, a patient should take these highly addictive medications.
4. He refused the narcotics per his wife and decided to fly four days postsurgery, despite his expert surgeon feeling his pain level during this time period warranted the use of narcotic medication.

Personally, I would call this a medically related fatal accident. What do you think?

I urge you to read the NTSB interviews of the pilot's wife and friends. This pilot seemed competent and thorough. This accident leaves more questions than answers. Maybe that is because in a thorough investigation, you often will have more questions than answers at the end.

THE TOXICOLOGY REPORT

Other than lidocaine, presumably given during the emergency treatment of this mortally injured pilot, there was no mention whatsoever of any narcotic or sedating medications.

The one thing this accident fully points out is that a properly conducted NTSB investigation may not include all the pertinent details in the final narrative, but it most definitely *should* include a full assessment of the pilot's medical history. This shouldn't occur only on those rare occasions when a pilot tells everyone he just had surgery. It should happen with *all* fatal accidents.

DEN06FA131

The next fatal accident killed two pilots in a Cirrus in Colorado when they encountered icing conditions.

Per the NTSB:

> The pilot's improper in-flight planning and decision making resulting in an inadvertent encounter with severe icing conditions during cruise flight and subsequent loss of aircraft control. Contributing factors include the pilot's failure to obtain a weather briefing, the thunderstorm, conditions conducive for structural icing, and the pilot's failure to deploy the parachute recovery system.

There is no evidence of a medical issue other than bad judgment.

This is the fourth incident where icing conditions are involved in a Cirrus fatal accident, as well as another case of failure to launch the emergency parachute. One wonders if there isn't an attitude that prevents a pilot from wanting to admit at an early enough instance that the emergency has progressed to the point that he needs to activate this device.

4

TREATING ALL VICTIMS THE SAME

DCA07MA003

IN 2006 A fairly famous incident occurred when a professional baseball player was killed along with his flight instructor while transiting down the East River in New York City. When they attempted to turn, they collided with an apartment building. They were killed, and three persons on the ground were injured.

This accident was the synthesis of my realizing this book wasn't about light sport or fatal Cirrus accidents at all. As I digested the reports on this accident, and while reading other accident reports, I realized that a larger topic was emerging. The NTSB doesn't seem to follow a set protocol for handling the *human* factors of an accident. However, they do appear to follow a script when handling and investigating the *mechanics* of accidents.

This is a large issue. Victims have the right to have their accidents investigated with equal vigor. Being injured because a millionaire baseball player runs into an apartment building should not be treated any differently than being killed when your less-well-known but far richer "friend" takes you into a mountain in an identical airframe while he or she is on cocaine and methamphetamines. Yet this accident was treated differently and in an inappropriate manner solely because of the publicity and not at all for the further advancement of aviation safety.

If you read the narrative, you will find fourteen names attached, including twelve government employees. That is about eight to ten more names than the normal Cirrus accident report has, which typically also includes two or three consultants from the manufacturers.

It is interesting how involved a person will get in an accident investigation if someone famous has died. When we look back at the three previous accidents narrative reports, we see listed hree government employees, two government employees, and two government employees, respectively. This is more the norm. The concept that everyone and their mothers got on board an accident investigation—simply because it was a high-profile event, when in fact, all victims have the same right to a true and full investigation—overlooks a simple fact: in the accident docket for the Manhattan crash, no apparent attempt to get medical records appears to have been undertaken. Even though twelve investigators were involved in the accident, not a bit of medical history appears in the docket. This indicates that the NTSB has no real policy in place clearly delineating the exploration of human factors. There were dozens of pages on radar plots, avionics, and so on. The sole bit of medical information placed in the docket was attachment seven: the toxicology screening.

The really sad part of this comes when we understand the two-part process of why this is an issue.

1. The NTSB has a checklist form driving the collection of other data. You can find examples of this checklist in numerous docket files for other accidents.
2. There is not apparently much of a checklist form annunciating each and every step for human factors data collection.
3. So, while you see an investigation of an accident often first focused on gathering all available wreckage together to begin piecing together the puzzle, you see a complete lack of any attempt

at all to gather all the available medical information about a pilot prior to piecing together the far far more puzzle of "human factors".

Thus, we seem to have an agency that is *highly* adept at investigating items that are responsible for 5 percent of all fatal accidents, while simultaneously being totally incompetent at regularly and fully assessing the issues that cause 95 percent of all the other fatal accidents. As a result of having no set protocols to ensure minimum standards of data collection, we end up with some very well done accident reports (driven often only by the presence of a drug on the tox screen that prompts the NTSB to look deeper), and we also end up with some extremely poorly investigated accidents wherein a gentleman will spend days in the hospital prior to expiring with no toxicology reports, no medical records, and no medical history ever even considered. Worse, we have accidents that are clearly and unequivocally medical, and the NTSB simply refuses to consider that even probable.

This is negligent. I shouldn't have to figure out that the NTSB isn't bothering to do full accident investigations while I am using it to figure out how many accidents are medically related. It is offensive to the extreme that this is exactly how I had the epiphany that the NTSB has a bipolar approach wherein the mechanical and avionic aspects are treated with a mania driven to explore the why and the what-if, while the far more common human factors are shrugged off with a "whatever."

Ironically, the NTSB's bipolar approach to accident investigations virtually ensures that it will never uncover a bipolar pilot off her meds. After all, if you stop at the toxicology screen and the pilot hasn't been taking her meds, your toxicology report won't find anything. Some common sense would cure this.

The other irony is that without any checklist for evaluating human factors, the NTSB frequently comments on humans not following checklists as being the cause of accidents. The probable cause of the NTSB wrecking its accident investigations, therefore, is its failure to bother making a checklist.

LAX07FA021

The next accident has all the aspects of "get-there-itis," and it resulted in the deaths of four people.

The airplane started out from Lake Tahoe, a bit later than the pilot originally had planned, as the plane had frost on it. If you have never heard of frost or aren't familiar with frost, let me use a simpler, smaller word: it had ice on it. This isn't snark, it is foreshadowing.

The instrument-rated pilot then apparently didn't bother to check weather. In fact, per the NTSB report:

At the conclusion of filing the flight plan, the specialist asked if the pilot needed any additional services. The pilot stated that, "It's beautiful weather so I got weather on board, and we're set." There was no record of the pilot obtaining a weather briefing from FSS or via direct user access terminal (DUAT) service for the accident flight.

THE PROBLEM

The airplane was equipped with an XM Satellite Weather System. According to the supplement in the pilot's operating handbook, the XM Satellite Weather System enhances situational awareness by providing the pilot with real-time, graphical weather information depicted on the MFD (multi-function display). The information is not an FAA-approved weather source.

The pilot's weather display didn't meet FAA standards for checking weather, and he was going to go flying on a day when his airplane warned him from the beginning to check the weather. His airplane had ice on it.

The pilot filed an IFR plan prior to departing Lake Tahoe. Then, after climbing to thirteen thousand feet, he canceled his IFR plan because it was not available to the controller and switched to VFR.

Further radio contact indicated he was warned of a restricted area and given vectors to avoid this area. Later still, mention is made of him failing to avoid the restricted area.

As the pilot approached weather, he again requested IFR and advised that he wanted to maneuver around thunder cells. The controller evidently neglected to mention reports of icing in the area he was planning to transit. Icing ultimately led to the accident.

There was a lot of swiss cheese on this accident. At the end of the day, four people died, all for lack of familiarity with the airframe, the area, and the weather. (See: the swiss-cheese model of accidents.)

The NTSB report mentions most of the cheese slices:

The National Transportation Safety Board determines the probable cause(s) of this accident as follows:

The pilot's inadequate weather evaluation and continued flight into forecasted icing conditions. Contributing to the severity of the accident was the pilot's failure to follow proper operating procedures and deploy the CAPS when the airplane entered a spin. The flight service specialist's failure to follow published procedures to provide adverse weather or forecast potential hazardous conditions along the intended route of flight, as well as the air traffic controller's failure to provide the pilot with radar-displayed weather information were factors.

So six slices, and none of them mentions a more obvious question: Did this pilot have the habit of being less than prepared when taking off on a cross-country? No weather briefing, no understanding of the restricted areas, and so on. Single incident or lifetime of attitude and worldview? The NTSB response seems to be: "Whatever…if we really cared, we could look into it, I guess." Lassitude as federal policy.

ATL07FA013

In this accident, two persons died during an instrument approach under IMC conditions at the end of a three-and-a-half-hour cross-country. The pilot survived. The NTSB sought a subpoena for any blood retained by the medical center where the pilot was treated, and this blood was tested by the FAA. It had no significant positive findings. Ironically, even though granted the authority to do so by Congress, at no time during this investigation did the NTSB evidently subpoena any of the other medical records of the pilot, not while he was in the hospital, and not prior to this period.

Why would you give up the opportunity to investigate a person's medical history by limiting a subpoena to a hospital to just the blood results? The hospital records are likely going to be a heck of a lot more informative.

Point to make: obviously, someone at the NTSB does actually realize they have the power of subpoena granted to them by federal law. Elsewhere, it will become obvious that they apparently quite often forget that they possess this power.

Probable Cause

The pilot's failure to maintain airspeed while maneuvering with a low ceiling in instrument flight conditions, resulting in an inadvertent stall, and collision with trees and the ground. Factors in the accident were the pilot's failure to follow the published missed approach procedures, and the airplane's checklist procedures for a balked landing.

Two Passengers Died

I have no idea why a full assessment of all pilot medical issues wasn't performed. You have two innocent fatalities involved, and yet a total lack of interest in investigating this crash thoroughly. In fact, I find it very odd. It wasn't as if no one knew what hospital he was in. It may be that they just never considered that a hospital admission is the key to all the past medical information about a person. The NTSB didn't follow a checklist, apparently; however, they cited "the pilot's failure to follow the published missed approach procedures, and the airplane's checklist procedures for a balked landing."

IRONY

If you don't have the basic medical knowledge to realize that a hospital admission will soon tell you exactly where to start getting a pilot's medical history, then you are simply clueless about how to investigate a person's medical history. The patient's primary-care doctor, insurance carrier, and medical history will almost always be partially present in a hospital admission record. And once the box is partly opened, you are 99 percent there. This is medical kindergarten. The NTSB used its power of subpoena to get 1 percent of the information and ignored the other 99 percent they had the legal right to gather. You have to either just not care or not know what you are doing in such a case. Either way, this is appalling.

In a world of interconnected computerized faxing systems, the cost of sending a request, obtaining the records, and reviewing the records is negligible. A competent physician could have a pilot's medical records filleted in about thirty minutes after receiving them. It is child's play, a very *young* child's play. It would be laughable if the NTSB were to rebut this book based on cost of getting medical records; pathetically laughable, since it wouldn't have cost more than a dollar or so. Also pathetic because it is exactly what they likely will attempt to claim. And I will state the obvious as well: if you actually bother to find out what is causing crashes, then you will save a lot of money because you will be able to figure out how to have fewer crashes, and thus you'll end up needing to have fewer investigations.

NYC07FA037

The next flight was also an IFR cross-country flight. This one originated in Atlanta and was landing in North Carolina. In this accident, the pilot, who had a prior history of angioplasty and coronary-artery disease, crashed during landing. The presence of a sedating antihistamine was found during the toxicology report, suggesting that this flight should never have occurred. A night IFR landing is not the time to be sedated or suffering from sleep disturbances or allergies.

LAX07FA062

It was mountainous terrain rather than a landing sequence that ended the next life. Again, IMC conditions prevailed, and again this was a cross-country flight. The crash was a result of multiple decisions by the pilot and resulted in her death.

Per the NTSB: "The pilot's failure to maintain terrain clearance during cruise flight while flying at night at an altitude to remain clear of clouds and icing conditions. Contributing to the accident were an inadequate weather evaluation, the clouds, icing conditions, and the dark night lighting conditions."

Swiss cheese.

The pilot's history of migraines was previously known to the FAA; no other attempts at obtaining medical records appears to have been done by the NTSB on this human-factors-based fatal accident. Again, though, IFR conditions at night in a high-performance aircraft. Moving on.

LET'S TALK SLEEP

The primary window of circadian low (WOCL) is a period of time known to some pilots and aviation medicine folks, but it is not a common term in everyday society. It is that period of time when your attention span, concentration, and detail orientation are at their nadir. It occurs around 2:00 a.m. and lasts until about 6:00 a.m. It is a fancy way of saying "sleepy time."

People fall asleep and die on the highway, they perform worse on shift work, they mishear information, and they make bad judgments during this time period at a higher rate than at other times of the day. It also has additive impacts when a person is up for several days in a row or has an issue with insomnia or is on medications such as Benadryl that interrupt deeper sleep.

For some interesting reading on this, please see www.faa.gov/documentLibrary/media/Advisory_Circular/AC%20117-3.pdf. Or simply type "primary WOCL" into Google.

I bring this up because the next accident is the classic story of a WOCL event.

NYC08FA041

The accident took place at 1:50 a.m. A pilot awoke around 6:30 a.m., went to work, and then flew to watch a family member compete in an athletic contest in Virginia that evening.

The accident happened on the return landing approach under IMC conditions. The first approach was missed, and the airplane initiated a missed approach and realigned itself. The crash occurred two miles short of the runway.

Toxicology was reportedly negative, and the narrative mentions an autopsy that asserts cause of death as blunt-force trauma. No attempt to collect medical records was mentioned.

The probable-cause report included pilot fatigue as a causative factor.

This accident gives us a couple of medical issues to consider: Fatigue? Sleep pattern? Workload? Previous recent medical history? Did he have a root canal three days ago, and did his dentist say, "Oh, just take ibuprofen"? Was he morbidly obese and never considered for sleep apnea?

A well-planned and dedicated accident assessment would include having the insight to consider that *most* accidents have a judgment and/or medical issue and thus require an assessment of these factors. This is what is missing. This accident also had two government employees involved on the final report listing, the primary investigator and the local Flight Standards District Office (FSDO) representative. There were two outside personnel consulted, one from the Cirrus corporation and one from the engine manufacturer. This is far different from the New York Cirrus crash involving a professional baseball player where over 10 federal employees jumped onto the bus for the photo-op disguised as an accident investigation.. This time around, evidently, there weren't a lot of opportunities for face time on the national news, which seems to factor into whether aviation accidents are taken seriously or not.

Assessing this accident from a mechanical basis seems like the last place I'd begin, but then, I am a physician, so perhaps my judgment is biased.

Now closely consider the next accident; things are about to be less cloudy.

CHI08FA039

This occurred in VFR conditions, less than three months after the previous accident. They are linked for several reasons. The most obvious is that they both occurred during aborted landings.

This accident took place at about 2:55 in the afternoon. It was also a cross-country flight, this one originating in South Dakota.

Four persons died during this accident, including the pilot, who was being treated for sleep apnea. His average daily CPAP usage prior to the accident was four hours per night, which is a bit under optimum but does indicate he was diligent about wearing his mask to sleep. Diligence is a sign of good judgment.

The pilot's medical certificate did have a limitation: "not valid for any class after…", he had a special issuance for sleep apnea.

Per the report: "He had been issued a FAA third-class medical certificate on July 25, 2007, through an Aviation Medical Examiner Assisted Special Issuance for obstructive sleep apnea with the limitation that it was not valid for any class after July 31, 2008."

This is a time to pause on this issue.

It is important to understand that my comments up to now are my opinions based solely on the information available from the NTSB records I have access to currently. This is important for several reasons.

1. In the event where three passengers and a pilot died, it is important not to slander or demean the decedents. The pilot may have had no other issues and in fact appears to have just passed a flight review and an instrument check within the same month as the accident.
2. It is important not to lead people down wrong pathways. Simple errors that are misunderstood, such as the report listing that there was no medical certificate when in fact there appears to have been one, is the type of miscommunication that can cause needless hurt to family members of either the passengers or the pilot, particularly if it shines an unflattering light on the pilot.
3. The importance of *full* data collection, then, illustrates how just such mistakes can be minimized.

I think this report illustrates just how important filling in the blanks regarding accidents is, and it also illustrates how filling in the blanks is not being done. I have no idea of this pilot's BMI, his fitness status, his last doctor visits, his most recent usage of medications, and so on. Sleep apnea can have a lot of comorbidity in a fifty-year-old pilot and *usually* is diagnosed when a pilot who is morbidly obese complains to his or her primary-care doctor about being tired a lot during the day. That doesn't mean that is the case with this pilot; however, when three people die and a government entity that knows most crashes are the result of human conditions claimed this accident was a result of human factors, it is important that you do your job thoroughly.

NTSB PROBABLE CAUSE

"The pilot not maintaining adequate airspeed for the gusty crosswind conditions and the stall/spin encountered during the go-around. Contributing to the accident were the crosswinds and wind gusts."

I want to return to the previous accident's probable cause for a moment to reflect on a set of comments within it.

NYC08FA041 REVISITED

Examination of the airplane did not reveal any preimpact malfunctions. The pilot woke up about 19 hours prior to the accident and the investigation revealed that he did not sleep between the start of his day and the accident.

Contributing to the accident were pilot fatigue and air traffic control's failure to issue a minimum safe altitude warning.

So what is my point?

This is actually very simple and very complex. It is complex if you missed the nuances, and it is simple if you didn't.

Let's read the full probable cause of the second accident:

The airplane's recorded airspeed indicated that the airplane slowed on final approach and subsequently encountered a recorded stall/spin condition during go-around from runway 12. A post impact ground fire and explosion occurred. The recorded winds at the airport were 190 degrees at 15 knots, gusting to 22 knots. On-scene and follow-up examinations of the wreckage and recorded data from the airplane's recoverable data module revealed no airplane or engine pre-impact anomalies. The maximum demonstrated crosswind component for the aircraft was 20 knots.

Subsequent to the accident a remark was entered to the airport's master record. The remark advised pilots landing on runway 12 to be alert for turbulence and possible wind shear when winds are out of the south.

The National Transportation Safety Board determines the probable cause(s) of this accident as follows:

The pilot not maintaining adequate airspeed for the gusty crosswind conditions and the stall/spin encountered during the go-around. Contributing to the accident were the crosswinds and wind gusts.

So?

Let's go back and look at the clues I have been placing for you:

1. I mentioned the primary WOCL in regard to the first accident.
2. I mentioned that the second accident occurred at about 2:55 p.m.
3. I mentioned the second pilot had sleep apnea.
4. I mentioned that four hours per night was a bit less than what we'd like to see for successful treatment. A good night's sleep requires seven to eight hours. I'd like to know the actual CPAP usage not just for the past three days but for the past month.
5. I mentioned that *most* people were diagnosed with sleep apnea owing to three factors: obesity, poor fitness, and daytime fatigue.

What should your first question be?

It might be: How many WOCLs are there? If there is a primary WOCL, are there others?

You might already know the answer, or you may have Googled it. The answer is yes. There is a secondary period of circadian low, characterized by a *decrease* in performance that gets worse the more sleep debt the person has.

Remember the vague precision of *about* 2:55 p.m.? The secondary WOCL is the period of midafternoon. During this time, sleepiness increases and performance decreases.

Sleep apnea is a disease characterized by daytime sleepiness. The pilot was being treated for a disease wherein the mistakes one makes during the secondary WOCL are amplified by the additive factors of increasing sleep debt.

How adequate was his treatment? The FAA likes to see at least six hours per night; he was averaging a lot less than that.

Who knows? The previous accident closed mentioning fatigue as a factor; however, for this accident, we have no idea if the concept of fatigue was even ever discussed or considered.

Someone had to have treated him for sleep apnea. He didn't wake up one day from a night of extremely poor sleep and stumble down to the local hardware store and hook himself up to a wet-dry vac.

Medical records should be a prerequisite for any accident investigation in aviation.

We cannot pretend to know that human factors are the most common causes of accidents while ignoring the importance of the medical history of a pilot.

It is a total disservice to the memory of the passengers of every single fatal aviation accident if we simply make a pretense of caring about accident causality. *Period.* I cannot say it any clearer than that.

LAX08FA043

In this accident, a forty-one-year-old pilot with no reported medical problems lost control over his Cirrus during a low pass over a friend's house, while trying to have a cell phone conversation with him in strong winds.

There is no review of other issues the pilot may have had. Clearly, this accident was a result of bad judgment. I'd like to know more about his past actions. You can't elucidate what you don't investigate.

DFW08FA060

This was a confusing crash. The NTSB reports that the seventy-two-year-old flight instructor, who had no apparent flight time in the model, was giving a biennial review to another pilot, the aircraft's owner. The probable cause report stated that the flight instructor stalled and crashed the aircraft during the return to the airport.

The report states that the aircraft began to enter a snap roll and then crashed. It is unclear how it was determined who was in control of the aircraft during that time, and the docket isn't available to search via the Internet. This may have been related to the data card on the avionics package, or perhaps I missed a nuance.

There was no apparent attempt made to collect any past medical information of any depth from either the owner or the instructor, both of whom died in the accident.

NYC08FA138

This occurred in night marginal VFR conditions during the initial climb. The pilot and passenger were killed after the aircraft impacted terrain. Why the pilot entered into a turning descent prior to impact doesn't appear to have been addressed by the NTSB. No discussion of the late-night departure, the impact of fatigue, a description of the pilot's previous week, or the pilot's medical history appears in the narrative. The fifty-four-year-old pilot and his son were killed. The toxicology report was negative. Sometimes NTSB will investigate; sometimes they won't. A checklist would fix this issue.

MIA08FA081

Diphenhydramine makes an appearance once again in the next crash. The warning about using this medication while performing complex tasks seems ignored far too often. The fifty-one-year-old pilot died during the landing sequence when he lost control of his complex aircraft. I'm calling this one medical. He was also on Ambien, another sedative. Medical records? Nope. Ambien requires a prescription, so it is a safe bet that one of the major US pharmacies had documentation of who was treating this pilot. It isn't that difficult to get information, you simply have to care.

The crash occurred at about 4:00 p.m. in VFR meteorological conditions at the end of a cross-country flight.

SEA08FA108

Mountainous terrain, VFR into IFR, and night conditions all played key roles in this accident, which killed a Cirrus pilot in California. The toxicology screening was negative, and no evidence of any attempt at gathering medical records made its way into the narrative report.

DFW08FA111

This one is shrouded in mystery. Speculation was that either incapacitation or fuel exhaustion led to the death of the fifty-four-year-old pilot and the two passengers. Toxicology was negative; no medical records are cited in the narrative. It would appear that lip service to the victims was given, but there really was no in-depth attempt to fully understand any human factors that might have been involved in this three-person fatal incident. As is often the case, an autopsy was not possible, making assessment of medical records of much greater importance. Review of the docket shows a minimalistic approach to figuring out this accident. After all, fuel exhaustion is possibly a *secondary* issue if the primary issue is that the pilot had a history of mental illness or sleep apnea or had multiple cardiac problems for which he wasn't seeking treatment. Did that pilot have any of these issues? If he did and failed to disclose it, this would have been a vehicular homicide investigation. But if you don't even bother to look, then you are going to miss more than a few homicides.

Unless you dig for information, you are fairly unlikely to find it. The accident docket of files is searchable. I would suggest reading through it and asking yourself, "Did we go to great trouble to find out the primary causes of this accident?" Certainly, we didn't spend the time and resources that were spent on the accident that killed one fewer person in Manhattan, and we certainly didn't see the involvement of twelve government employees listed on the final narrative, which raises the question: In a representative form of government, when did three lives become of less investigative value than two?

The comments of witness number two are interesting. He stated that the pilot verbalized that he had a strong disinclination toward pulling the ballistic parachute. This bears consideration, as it isn't going to be the only time we see people killed after this comment occurred.

Reflect on this: the pilot told people that he was going to fly an airplane that had equipment designed to save his life but that he had no intention of using said equipment.

LAX08FA265B

This flight was involved in a midair collision with a Cessna 172. No medical cause was found by the NTSB.

CHI08FA282

IMC conditions and landing once again become the centerpieces of this accident, in which two customers, as well as the commercial pilot, were killed.

ERA09FA053

This was another IMC night landing to end a long cross-country, beginning in Ohio and ending with two fatalities and three injuries in Tallahassee, Florida. The toxicology report on the sixty-four-year-old pilot was negative. There were no medical records listed in the docket reports. The pilot neglected to remove the safety tag hanging from the emergency parachute handle.

Again, this points to a question: Did the pilot use good judgment? We know he neglected or intentionally ignored one part of the preflight without question. But what was his overall judgment like? We have no idea, because we see no real attempt to look at the human factors that cause most accidents. We do know that he had flown a four-and-a-half-hour flight. We do not know his overall fitness level, his sleep habits, or his previous medical conditions; nor do we know anything about the presence or absence of medical conditions. No interviews of his instructors appear to have been done.

We have only this:

The pilot's failure to maintain adequate airspeed on final approach, which resulted in a low-altitude aerodynamic stall and spin. Contributing to the accident was the pilot's failure to fly the published instrument approach and his subsequent failure to execute a timely missed approach.

Yes, but *why?*

ERA09FA148

The next flight was another midafternoon crash on approach. This was under VFR conditions. There was a loss of aircraft control during the landing approach for undetermined reasons.

The autopsy report wasn't included in the docket, and the toxicology report was negative. No medical reports were obtained, no interviews of family members regarding sleep/wake cycle, pain syndromes, or other psychiatric issues were obtained. There was a report by the pilot of smelling smoke in the cockpit. It was the second time in a month this had occurred. However, an extremely thorough review by the NTSB on the mechanics and avionics failed to show any mechanical issues. Juxtaposed with the dearth of medical information gathering, this is a stark contrast, particularly when the probable cause report is essentially a shrugging of one's shoulders.

CEN09FA146

A night VFR flight ended in the death of three persons in Wisconsin. The accident occurred at 7:00 p.m. after darkness had set in, and the pilot had some Benadryl in his system. This would suggest he had difficulty sleeping the prior evening, had a cold, or had allergies. We aren't able to tease out any of these issues because there was no attempt by the NTSB to find out *why* he was taking a medication that has sedating properties and can impact sleep quality and thus performance for extended periods of time. The accident's probable-cause report? Well, it wasn't really too specific.

To wit: "The pilot's failure to maintain control of the airplane while flying at night in instrument meteorological conditions."

Three people died.

The narrative stated twice that it was VFR night conditions. The probable IMC conditions: possibly an oversight, just as one might consider it an oversight to not fully assess human factors in an accident resulting in three deaths. We all make mistakes; we must focus on the systemic mistakes.

ERA09FA169

This is a flight instruction event wherein two pilots were killed in Florida. The toxicology report was negative for both pilots, and the autopsies were not cited regarding significant medical issues. However, an overview of the major injuries with an autopsy diagram is present in the thirty-page survivability documents of the docket. The deceased were twenty-three and thirty years of age.

If one applies the swiss-cheese model of causative factors to accidents, perhaps one should know not to take a swiss-cheese approach to investigating accidents, hoping one gets lucky and the holes line up.

There are holes lining up in the cheese, but someone didn't bother getting the slices all collected. We have no idea if they would have aligned or not. Read the following cherry-picked items from NTSB reports, and do some careful reflection.

MY CHERRY-PICKING

1. "On February 17, 2009, at 1418 eastern standard time, a Cirrus SR20, N493DA, call sign Connection 424, registered to Boston Aviation Leasing II LLC, and operated by Delta Connection Academy (DCA) as a 14 Code of Federal Regulations Part 91 instructional flight, was substantially damaged when it collided with trees and terrain in Deltona, Florida."

2. "Two witnesses in the same neighborhood stated they were checking their mail between 1430 and 1500, when they heard an airplane flying overhead. They observed the airplane flying eastbound between 225 to 250 feet above the trees."

3. "Delta Connection personnel notified the on duty Delta Academy Manager at 1930 that the airplane was overdue. The Federal Aviation Administration (FAA) issued an alert aircraft notification at 2153."

4. "At 1417:34, the airplane was at 3,131 feet heading 064 degrees, the engine rpm had increased to 2,500 rpm, the indicated airspeed was 54 knots, and the ground speed was 52 knots. The airplane entered a left hand spin at 1417:35, and the recorded primary flight display data ends at 1418:02."

5. "The pilot had flown 7.4 hours in the last 24 hours, of which 2.5 hours were in the SR20."
6. "The flight was scheduled from 1330 to 1530. According to information provided by DCA, the flight was extended until 1930 at an undetermined time."

PROBABLE CAUSE FINDINGS

"The pilot receiving instruction's failure to maintain adequate airspeed while maneuvering, which resulted in an aerodynamic stall and subsequent loss of control. Contributing to the accident was the flight instructor's inadequate supervision and both pilots' failure to deploy the ballistic parachute at a higher altitude."

DEEP IN THE DOCKET DOCUMENTS

The airplane was found at 3:45 the next morning by sheriff's helicopter using infrared, which showed two bodies emitting heat, not moving, within the cockpit.

OK, so what do we know, and what can we be left to wonder?

If the pilot has 7.4 hours within the past twenty-four hours (which is likely a math error, since twenty-four-hour periods are rolling consecutive hours for purposes of staying within the regulations), then it would have possibly been illegal for him to flight instruct about half an hour of takeoff, owing to federal regulations that limit the instructor to eight hours in the past twenty-four. I'd like to know if he *truly* was at 7.4 hours in the past rolling twenty-four hours when the flight originated (which would possibly make the flight illegal thirty-six minutes after takeoff). Then I'd like to know if this was a pattern.

I'd like to know the times of origin for all the previous flights in the past twenty-four hours, to see if in fact he was only thirty-six minutes away from violating federal law in an aircraft that was alleged at one time to be scheduled until 3:30 but then for some reason, without any explanation, was changed to 7:30.

There is a "convenience" factor for the flight school to say the airplane was scheduled until 7:30 p.m., if in fact it was supposed to be back at 3:30 p.m. The accident occurred at 2:18 p.m., yet the school didn't start contacting people until after 7:00 p.m. If I were a lawyer, I'd ask, "How do you not know your training aircraft are missing five hours after an accident?" The answer? "Well, it was scheduled until 7:30, so we had no reason to be suspicious."

The problem with that logic is, would this have put the pilot in violation of federal law? He was at 7.4 hours at the start of the flight. The flight was scheduled for a 3:30 return. It wrecked at 2:18. If he had flown until the new scheduled time of 7:30, would this or would this not have placed him in violation?

This question is important, because it highlights some possibilities that we need to think about.

1. Did the flight school change the scheduling *after* the fact to protect itself from legal liability regarding a missing aircraft not being reported for four hours *after* it was originally scheduled to return? Is that fraud, and is it criminal when two deaths are involved?
2. *How close* was the pilot to violating federal law, and would the *changed* schedule have caused him to do so?
3. Did the school track instructors' hours to protect itself from such a violation, and what was the school's legal role in ensuring instructors *didn't* overshoot federal regulations?

These would be crucial questions if a student's family were seeking legal remedy for the loss of a loved one. It also could relate to criminality.

If the NTSB is tasked with making recommendations for improving safety, and it found a flight school committing federal crimes as a result of the thoroughness of its investigation, then it would truly make an impact on future aviation safety, one would surmise.

Let's add some more questions to the mix.

When an infrared system finds two warm objects, are those objects living or dead? And if dead, how long will they be hot on the infrared? This is important because of time of death and toxicology.

If the pilots were alive but unconscious when they were discovered at 3:00 a.m., then their toxicology was thirteen hours beyond the time of the accident. This has implications for the utility of the toxicology report as a starting point for investigation and points to why a far better point of origin for investigating medical issues is the insurance billing and the doctor office notes on a person.

It also adds nuance to the discussion of whether a flight school is or is not culpable for knowing fairly quickly when one of its airplanes wrecks. The airplane was originally scheduled to return one hour after the time of the wreck, but this scheduling was changed to magically match the period of time when the school actually reported it missing. This could be coincidence, but it walks like a duck. Maybe I have just watched too many early-morning detective shows. It makes me go *hmmmmmmm*.

CEN09FA267

April 28, 2009 saw two people die in a Cirrus during an afternoon take-off into IMC conditions. Some clues to this loss of control stall/spin event can be gleaned from the NTSB narrative report.

CLUE #1

Data recovered from the primary flight display also included the inbound flight into CGF. The pilot executed 3 missed approaches in an attempt to land at CGF. He was able to successfully land following the 4th approach. The first approach began about 1234. On each approach, the autopilot successfully captured the localizer course inbound to the runway.

CLUE #2

The CGF air traffic control tower (ATCT) issued a takeoff clearance for the flight from Runway 6 at 1611, instructing the pilot to fly the runway heading and climb to 3,000 feet mean sea level (msl).

The controller observed the airplane take off and enter the clouds. Takeoff and initial climb appeared to be normal. At 1612, the controller instructed the pilot to contact departure control. The pilot acknowledged the instruction; however, the pilot never established communications with the departure controller. At 1614, the pilot transmitted "we're having trouble getting" on the CGF tower frequency.

At 1615, the pilot transmitted "having trouble mike delta." There were no subsequent transmissions from the pilot. At 1616, the departure controller relayed a low altitude alert in the blind to the accident flight.

So we know that the crash sequence began within three minutes of takeoff, and we can reasonably assume part of the issue was that the pilot was having a radio communications distraction while departing into weather. We also know from his first four attempts at landing at the runway that the combination of the weather, the equipment, and the pilot demonstrated a high potential for something bad happening. It wasn't going to take much to set this off. It is also reasonable to assume an added mental stress load internally with the pilot, owing to the issues he had with landing.

The toxicology screening was negative, the pilot was aged fifty-one, and a passenger died. The pilot's most recent flight information appears not to have been available. The NTSB probable-cause panel indicated that the pilot was at fault and didn't maintain adequate control of the aircraft while in IMC conditions and while trying to perform cockpit tasking, such as setting up the autopilot properly.

I would also presume that his failure to take the course on IFR transition to the Cirrus seven months earlier, opting only for the VFR transition, may have also been a significant factor and may shed light on his decision-making process to take off into IMC.

The estate sued Cirrus. Ironic, since it was the pilot who chose not to take Cirrus IFR transition training. But then, if we want truth, a courtroom probably isn't our best place to look. If I were part of the family of the twenty-six-year-old victim of the accident, I'd probably sue the estate of the individual who had so much difficulty landing in bad weather, who didn't bother with the IFR transition course, and who the NTSB stated didn't control the aircraft.

CEN09FA363

This accident was a 10:00 p.m. landing incident after a cross-country flight with multiple legs that originated at noon. It occurred in night instrument conditions, killing the sixty-year-old pilot. The toxicology report showed evidence of Oxazepam, a highly addictive benzodiazepine used for anxiety. This medication is not legal to use when flying aircraft, particularly if taken on a daily basis.

This is an excerpt from the Physician's Desk Reference:

WARNINGS/PRECAUTIONS
May impair mental/physical abilities. Withdrawal symptoms (dysphoria, insomnia, convulsions, tremor, abdominal/muscle cramps, vomiting, sweating) reported after abrupt discontinuation of therapy. Avoid abrupt discontinuation and follow gradual dosage-tapering schedule after extended therapy. Carefully monitor addiction-prone individuals (eg, drug addicts, alcoholics); predisposed to habituation and dependence. Hypotension reported rarely; administer with caution to patients in whom a drop in BP might lead to cardiac complications (especially in the elderly). Caution in elderly.

ADVERSE REACTIONS
Drowsiness, dizziness, vertigo, headache, transient amnesia, memory impairment.[1]

What we know so far: the pilot had a long day; it was late at night; he *may* have had a sleeping disorder or an anxiety disorder; and he was taking a medication that is highly addictive, has withdrawal symptoms, causes sleepiness, and isn't legal to fly with. It is reasonable to assume it wasn't reported on his flight medical.

Continuing on: "The pilot's failure to maintain airspeed which resulted in a loss of aircraft control during a go-around. Factors associated with the accident were the dark night lighting conditions, moderate to heavy rain, and fatigue."

That was the probable-cause finding. Let's look at the docket and see if the toxicology and the length of the flight spurred a deeper exploration into the pilot's medical or social history. First, let us refresh the basic points of what we know in a bulleted list.

1. Toxicology shows a prescription drug.
2. FAA medical didn't show this drug use.
3. The drug is highly addictive.
4. The drug sedates.
5. The drug requires a physician to prescribe it.
6. The NTSB recognized fatigue as a factor in this accident.

OK, off to the NTSB docket search; cue the crickets.

This accident begs for a search of past medical records, if for nothing else, then out of fairness to the deceased. He has a medication that when inappropriately used is a grounding medication. The NTSB raises the issue but doesn't put it to bed. If the pilot had a legitimate reason for this medication, it would be insulting to his family for the NTSB to hint that the use was illicit. Yet that is what a passing mention does. It

---

1 http://www.pdr.net/drug-summary/Oxazepam-oxazepam-1581.

nuances the report so that any objective person would raise an eyebrow. If the eyebrow is left raised by the NTSB's refusal to do its job, then that is disgraceful.

A competent investigation would say, "An evaluation of this medication usage shows that the pilot used it for muscle spasms in the previous week," or "His medical records show no prescription charged to his insurance or prescribed by his primary-care doctor, and his family denies any bottles with prescription medication in his home." Both of these sentences show a dedication to the concept of "investigation" versus the concept of "oh, well."

I would further add that getting this information is remarkably simple. You have to both know how and want to do it. The NTSB has shown that on occasion it does know how to get the information. It has also shown an overwhelmingly obvious disinclination toward wanting to get such information.

ERA09FA429

This accident, which happened in West Virginia, contains an immediate clue about incapacitation.

Per the NTSB: Instrument meteorological conditions prevailed, and an instrument flight rules (IFR) flight plan was filed for the Title 14 Code of Federal Regulations Part 91 personal flight. The flight originated at York Municipal Airport (JYR), York, Nebraska, about 1840, and was bound for Eagle Creek Airpark (EYE), Indianapolis, Indiana.

Should we look at a map? Nebraska is far closer to Indiana than West Virginia, so the pilot overshot Indy by a fairly significant amount of miles.

This accident was a hypoxia event, but it was a medical arrogance/judgment event as well. The pilot had had issues with high-altitude hypoxia in this airplane previously and had also installed, without following FAA protocols, an oxygen system.

He additionally used a mask that wasn't approved for the system. Also, despite the new system, he had continued to have issues with hypoxia while flying the airplane on previous trips. It was noted that he didn't use the pulse oximeter regularly that was present on the airplane. A pulse oximeter will tell you what your current oxygenation status is, and good ones have both a blinking light and an audible signal when your oxygen levels are too low.

Unfortunately, since the toxicology report was negative, the NTSB docket does not include other possibly pertinent medical records. This was a sixty-six-year-old man dying of hypoxia after making repeated decisions to place himself into a hypoxic situation without exercising due caution. Yeah, I'm thinking I'd be interested in what else was in this pilot's medical history.

The NTSB report remarks that this accident was a result of a man deciding to modify a system on his own. Despite the modifications he had noted, he still had hypoxia occurring. And yet, rather than fix the issue, he flew repeatedly into the brink—I'd say the brink of sanity.

Had his physician advised him to use psychiatric medications? Given his choices, it wouldn't seem unreasonable. Was he refusing to take these psychiatric medications? That would certainly explain his negative toxicology screen.

Am I being mean? No, not at all. The word is *thorough*. Alzheimer's isn't a myth; it happens. Cops kill kids every year who have schizophrenia and who are off their medications. This isn't hyperbole; it is fact. Alzheimer's sufferers and schizophrenics who are not on medications both have negative toxicology results.[2]

According to the *Washington Post*, more than 125 mentally ill persons were killed by police in the first half of 2015 alone. I'll wager you that their toxicology reports aren't going to show that they were being adequately treated, but that hardly means they would have been safe to

---

2 https://www.washingtonpost.com/national/final-tally-police-shot-and-killed-984-people-in-2015/2016/01/05/3ec7a404-b3c5-11e5-a76a-0b5145e8679a_story.html.

fly airplanes. The point I am making is: toxicology screenings at autopsy aren't the end-all, be-all the NTSB often seems to think they are.

ERA09FA515

This accident gives away the medical reason quite early, but it is subtle:

PERSONNEL INFORMATION

The pilot, age forty-nine, held a private pilot certificate, with a rating for airplane single-engine land.

According to Federal Aviation Administration (FAA) records, the pilot received his private pilot certificate on November 21, 2008. Review of the pilot's logbook revealed entries beginning on March 16, 2008, through August 22, 2009, for approximately 368 hours of total flight experience, of which about 333 hours were logged as "dual received."

Did you catch it?

Always look for the "weird." It seems a bit strange that a pilot doesn't want to fly alone occasionally. To have 333 hours of *instruction* is a sign of something. It is an outlier. Let's jump to the end of the movie and read the probable-cause report:

The pilot had a history of attention deficit disorder and depression (both previously treated with medications) and of anxiety (for which he had previously been hospitalized and for which he had been prescribed a potentially impairing medication for use "as needed"). None of this information had been reported to the Federal Aviation Administration. The pilot was at risk (but had not been evaluated) for obstructive sleep apnea because of his history of snoring, obesity, and high blood pressure. It is possible that the pilot was experiencing symptoms of his unreported mental conditions, that he was fatigued due to undiagnosed obstructive sleep apnea, or that he had recently used an anti-anxiety medication at the time of the accident. While it is possible that impairment from one or more of those sources could have adversely impacted his performance during the accident sequence, the investigation was unable to determine the role that impairment may have played in the accident.

The National Transportation Safety Board determines the probable cause(s) of this accident as follows:

The pilot's failure to maintain aircraft control and altitude while maneuvering after takeoff.

Did I miss something?

Let's back up a bit and read some of the probable-cause report again:

The pilot had a history of attention deficit disorder and depression (both previously treated with medications) and of anxiety (for which he had previously been hospitalized and for which he had been prescribed a potentially impairing medication for use "as needed"). None of this information had been reported to the Federal Aviation Administration. The pilot was at risk (but had not been evaluated) for obstructive sleep apnea because of his history of snoring, obesity, and high blood pressure. It is possible that the pilot was experiencing symptoms of his unreported mental conditions, that he was fatigued due to undiagnosed obstructive sleep apnea, or that he had recently used an anti-anxiety medication at the time of the accident. While it is possible that impairment from one or more of those sources could have adversely impacted his performance during the accident sequence, the investigation was unable to determine the role that impairment may have played in the accident.

Well, that seems a bit weird.

Is the NTSB saying they are not as good at accident investigation as some random doctor is?

What I mean is: I know the *exact* role this person's condition played in this accident. This accident *would never have happened* if the pilot had been fully evaluated by the FAA, if he had been honest, and if he hadn't been mentally ill. This pilot was flying illegally, and he certainly would have known that.

If he had followed the law, the airplane's ignition would have never turned that day, and thus I know *exactly* what role his condition played. His condition of being dishonest and being unfit to fly but ignoring those facts is what caused his death.

Further, if you can't figure out that a dishonest person with morbid obesity, depression, and anxiety is impaired, then perhaps you aren't as good an investigator as a random person we simply ask on the street.

5

Fact-Checking the Facts

CEN13FA558

I<small>N</small> <small>THIS</small> <small>CRASH</small>, which occurred in the parking lot of a bank, a sixty-three-year-old pilot and his wife were killed after he failed a downwind landing at an airport where he had never landed before. During his aborted go-around, he stalled and crashed. There was absolutely no medical information mentioned in the NTSB docket information.

CEN13FA456

In August 2013, two persons were killed in night IMC conditions. In this accident, there was mention of the pilot being on two medications that are of interest.

To wit:

Ephedrine detected in liver, ephedrine detected in blood (cavity), pseudoephedrine detected in liver, pseudoephedrine detected in blood (cavity), trimethoprim detected in liver, and trimethoprim detected in blood (cavity). Pseudoephedrine is used to relieve nasal congestion caused by colds, allergies, and hay fever. It is also used to temporarily relieve sinus congestion and pressure. Trimethoprim may be used for cold symptoms as well.

Trimethoprim is a prescribed antibiotic.

The questions become these: Why was this pilot on a prescribed antibiotic? Who prescribed it? What other medical issues did he have? How severe were his symptoms? None of these questions appear to have ever been asked. This very easily could have been a medically caused crash, but owing to no mechanism requiring a full examination of the causative human factors, we may never know. It is safe to assume he didn't magically obtain the antibiotic; he likely went to a pharmacy close to his house.

CEN13FA002

IMC conditions also prevailed in October 2012, when two more people were killed.

Clues are dropped in the final narrative report:

A certified flight instructor (CFI), who flew training flights with the accident pilot, stated that the pilot often struggled to maintain instrument flying proficiency due to an active lifestyle. He stated that the accident pilot was challenged with accomplishing routine instrument flying tasks, such as changing a radio control frequency while conducting an instrument approach.

And this:

On October 5, 2012, an autopsy was performed on the pilot by the Lake County Coroner. The cause of death was blunt force injuries. Toxicology testing of vitreous as part of the autopsy indicated past use of cocaine and hydrocodone. The FAA's Civil

Aeromedical Institute in Oklahoma City, Oklahoma, performed toxicology tests on the pilot, which was limited by the lack of available blood or urine. No ethanol was detected in the muscle or liver.

Trace amounts of tetrahydrocannabinol (marijuana) was found in lung and its metabolite tetrahydrocannabinol carboxylic acid was detected in the lung and liver.

This was a medically related crash. And it is clear that his lifestyle most likely did make it difficult to maintain proficiency.

Not only that, the toxicology report for the pilot isn't even in the accident docket. The toxicology report listed in the docket is not the pilot's. It is the *passenger's*.

> 0.0138 (ug/ml, ug/g) Tetrahydrocannabinol (Marihuana) detected in Lung
>> .0449 (ug/ml, ug/g) Tetrahydrocannabinol Carboxylic Acid (Marihuana) detected in Liver
>> .0087 (ug/ml, ug/g) Tetrahydrocannabinol Carboxylic Acid (Marihuana) detected in Lung

So given the absence of a pilot's toxicology report in the docket, and the fact that it appears the NTSB investigator used the passengers' toxicology report to determine that the pilot wasn't likely impaired, you can see that this accident wasn't properly investigated at all.

Additionally, as the narrative report stated, "The FAA's Civil Aeromedical Institute in Oklahoma City, Oklahoma, performed toxicology tests on the pilot, which was limited by the lack of available blood or urine."

So the investigation has no real ability to see what levels of cocaine, hydrocodone, and marijuana were in the pilot's body, only that there *were* such medications present.

You don't need anything more than the instructor's impression and the fact that the pilot used illegal medications to know this was a medical accident. It is obvious.

What did the NTSB's final report on probable cause conclude?

Examination of the airframe and engine did not reveal any pre-impact failures or malfunctions that would have precluded normal operation. Toxicology testing indicated the pilot used cocaine, hydrocodone, and marijuana at some point in the recent past. However, the use of the cocaine and hydrocodone likely did not affect the pilot's performance at the time of the accident, and the effect of the marijuana use could not be determined from the available evidence.

Bizarre. The NTSB investigators aren't saying that they couldn't determine if the drugs impaired the pilot. Instead, with absolutely no way of knowing, they are saying that the three drugs, two of which are illegal, likely didn't impair the pilot. How do you determine something didn't likely impair a pilot, when you have zero idea of what level of illegal drugs he was actually on?

That is beyond idiotic; it smells. Bad. Especially since the narrative report states the toxicology reports were "limited by the lack of available blood or urine."

How does an investigator state with any seriousness that when you have no blood or urine to test, and you know a pilot was taking hydrocodone, marijuana, and cocaine, that these drugs were likely not impairing him? Two of them are always illegal. You had no blood to test.

There is a huge difference between saying you *can't determine* if drugs are impairing and saying, as this investigator did, that the three drugs this pilot was illegally flying with in his system were *likely* not impairing.

One of the statements shows you aren't sure; the other suggests that you are. How do you become sure that three illegal drugs in a pilot's system are likely not impairing him when you have no blood levels to even assess? This investigation on an extremely rich pilot smells dirty.

We have a pilot who we know uses illegal drugs, including two that cause sedation, and now we have a person stating that two of these drugs likely had nothing to do with the crash? People who use cocaine on Tuesday evening don't usually get enough sleep. Flying on Wednesday evening could then amplify their fatigue level. People who use narcotics either do it for pain or for recreation. If they use the drug for recreation, they are often addicted and suffer severe withdrawal symptoms. If they use it for pain, guess what happens when it wears off? *Pain.*

Let us dig into the docket and see how the NTSB could possibly have concluded that a pilot whose judgment was so poor as to use two illegal drugs and possibly a third (the hydrocodone may have been prescribed) somehow has the sound mind and judgment to fly in IFR conditions at night when his own instructor stated he wasn't that great at doing it.

Cue the crickets. There is no full discussion of the medical records; there is no autopsy even listed. The toxicology report from the FAA indicates marijuana usage.

There is zero evidence given from a medical person that these medications and the pilot's usage of them contributed to the accident. It appears this was simply a guess. My probable cause is it is 100 percent illegal to fly with illegal drugs in your system. This crash therefore was clearly medical.

Another point—the narrative report stated that the tests were not done on the pilot's blood because of a lack of blood available. Based on not having blood levels, how is the NTSB saying it is likely that the three judgment-altering drugs weren't likely impairing him when he made the bad judgment to fly beyond his skill set?

Where are the medical records and interviews showing that he likely partied two weeks ago and not the night before? They aren't there.

Further, is this accident report a case where the NTSB even consulted with its own medical staff? Because if so, the process of placing the medical report into the docket seems flawed. Also, if NTSB medical staff members were consulted in this accident, I believe this proves they were incompetent.

There is zero probability that this wasn't a medical accident, as witnessed by the pilot's arrogant disregard for his health and his arrogant disregard for law and his arrogant inability to maintain competency in the airframe—as testified to by his instructor in this very NTSB report. The concept that you can divorce decision making that occurs in a pilot's *brain*, the major organ of life, from medical causation is simply nonsensical. There are more than enough pieces of evidence, even with just a shallow attempt at digging for the truth, to make the probable cause: pilot impairment by virtue of his history of life choices.

Perhaps the NTSB's understanding of "probable cause" is simply that if there is *no* probability that this accident was *anything* but a medically caused accident, this means they have to say they can find no probable cause. Since they don't write definitive-cause panels, this seems logical in an *Alice through the Looking Glass* Jabberwocky world gone madder.

I would also ask you to consider whether to connect the dots:

- The passengers' toxicology report made it onto the docket.
- The pilot's didn't.
- The pilot was taking hydrocodone, marijuana, and cocaine.
- There are no medical records on why he might be on the hydrocodone.
- There is no discussion of any attempt to get medical records or to discuss this case with the NTSB's own medical personnel.
- There was no blood sample or urine sample on the pilot, per the narrative report.
- The investigator stated not that he couldn't determine the extent the illegal drugs impaired the pilot; he instead stated, without any clarification, that is was *unlikely* that these illegal drugs impaired the pilot.

Does that smell to anyone else?

CEN12FA633

Five people died in this accident. All were on board the four-seat air-plane. The accident occurred in IMC conditions. There is little hint in the narrative about any real cause that killed this forty-four-year-old pi-lot and four others. The probable cause report lists spatial disorienta-tion. The accident docket lists no autopsy report, no medical records, no family interviews. There is a brief assessment of the fact there were five people in a four-seat aircraft, but the words *weight* and *balance* never occur in either document. In the docket reports, there is no discussion of the deceased passengers in any detail. This is the largest tragedy of all. It is as if their deaths have no relationship to the need for a thor-ough investigation, when, in fact, I would submit that these four people's deaths are the *only* reason for any NTSB investigation. Public safety and the NTSB's role in protecting the public in the future add value to these investigations. And to not even look into the issue or reflect on it other than a casual mention of five people in a four-seat plane is insulting to the public and these people's memory.

A Google search of the pilot and the accident shows far more than the NTSB investigation: three of the passengers were the fifteen-, six-teen-, and ten-year-old children of the pilot.

You don't fly five people in a four-seat aircraft. You especially don't fly two teenagers and a ten-year-old at night in instrument conditions in a four-seat aircraft with a fifth passenger. Some things are obviously poor judgment. The evidence is hard to argue with. The evidence is the gravestones. I am calling this a medical judgment issue: knowingly exceeding an aircraft's design while endangering your passengers in the process.

ERA12FA540

In this accident, the flight instructor took over the controls of the air-craft, and there was possible confusion over who was actually in control of the airplane. Insufficient altitude existed for the indecision that was apparently present. The aircraft was destroyed, the flight instructor was killed, and the student had no memory of the event. Besides a strong potential for fatigue and possible issues with the employers, there is no clear medical or judgment issue that the NTSB appeared to discover that could be considered pathological.

WPR12FA305

This flight, in which two persons were killed, occurred in Utah. Toxicology was not performed because of extreme decay. The NTSB narrative stated that no medical issues could be determined. The accident docket doesn't show any attempt to obtain medical records. The fifty-nine-year-old non-instrument-rated pilot evidently entered IFR conditions and appears to have become disoriented.

ERA12FA438

Another cross-country VFR into IMC crash occurred in Tennessee. The non-instrument-rated pilot expired. His toxicology screening was negative.

Per the narrative:

> According to an employee at NQA who talked to the pilot prior to departing on the accident flight, the pilot stated that he was in a "hurry to depart due to possible bad weather in the area." In addition, there was a weather briefing station located inside the fixed based operator at the departure airport; however, no airport personnel recalled the pilot using it on the day of the accident.

The pilot was witnessed being in a rush. Pilot's medical records per the docket: cue the crickets.

WPR12FA235

Sometimes a person's sociopathic behavior telegraphs the homicides he commits. This may have been the case in this accident, in which an airplane that was two-hundred-plus pounds overweight couldn't make it over the cliff it ran into. The clues that a homicide was soon to happen were present.

Per the NTSB report:

Elite Aviation rented the airplane to the pilot. A post-accident interview with their management personnel revealed that the pilot refueled the airplane at their facility. He then taxied the airplane to another area on the airport to load his passengers and baggage. This location was about 0.25 miles away from the Elite facility, and was not visible from their business. Elite personnel also reported that on a previous occasion, which occurred just after the accident pilot had been checked out in the airplane, he was observed loading the airplane for a flight. Elite management personnel noticed that the airplane would be overweight, at which time the pilot was informed that he could not take that much baggage on the flight.

Also during the interview, Elite management personnel revealed that the accident pilot would always try to circumvent things with the female office receptionists, but not with any of the male office personnel. In one instance, it was described that the accident pilot mentioned to the wife of one of the company's owners that he could fly the rental airplane without renter's insurance; the company co-owner said that this was not true. Elite personnel also reported that there were a few times when the accident pilot attempted to bargain airplane rental fees.

Cutting corners has no business in aviation.

Way too many deaths prove that it happens too often. This gentleman cut corners, ignored safety, and wasn't competent in the airframe or the conditions; thus, his sociologically significant poor judgment led to his death and three homicides.

ERA12FA303

If you aren't paying extra close attention to every detail, you can easily miss a nuance. This may have occurred with this South Carolina fatal accident.

Nuance one: the pilot had more than two hundred hours in the aircraft. He had never soloed the airplane until the day he died. This sounds familiar, doesn't it? We've seen one of these already, so we know how important it is to look at his medical history fully. Look back at ERA09FA515; this issue is a red flag. These two accidents happened within three years of each other in the same state. There is a disconnect here that demonstrates a lack of consistency in completing accident investigations.

Nuance two: the toxicology report stated he had no Nadolol in his blood, but he did have it in his urine.

The NTSB probable cause panel found the following:

> Review of the pilot's flight logs showed that he had accumulated more than 330 total hours of flight experience, including more than 220 hours in the accident airplane; however, he had not previously flown the accident airplane solo before the accident flight. Review of autopsy and toxicology test results showed no evidence of any preexisting condition that would have been expected to result in the pilot's incapacitation.

Despite this, I am going to call this probably medical, simply because there is something too abnormal about a pilot who doesn't fly solo for two hundred hours until the day he dies flying solo. It begs a full investigative effort. The begging continues to this day.

He had recently taken diphenhydramine, and it was present in his urine but not his blood. He also was taking a BPH medication as well as a gastric reflux medication. We know, then, that he had at least four medical conditions: (1) reflux, (2) insomnia and/or allergies, (3) prostatic hypertrophy, and (4) hypertension or some other need for Nadolol, of which there are several.

So what are we missing? Nadolol for hypertension should be taken daily, so it should be present in the blood. If it isn't being taken for hypertension, then why else would you take it? There are several reasons, including different cardiac issues and a few neurological concerns. Now, it could be hypertensive therapy, and the pilot missed a dose. So why was he on Nadolol?

Here are my issues: you have a pilot on a medication; he is possibly not taking it daily. Its main use is daily for hypertension. There is no report of whether this information was ever provided in an FAA medical examination. An autopsy is mentioned, but no autopsy report is in the accident docket. This simply isn't acceptable. The total lack of medical reports from the treating doctor for this patient is also disappointing. The lack of clarity is a strong indication that there is also a lack of a protocol.

CEN12FA251

Instrument conditions prevailed in this next accident. The fifty-nine-year-old pilot died on a flight from New Jersey bound for Ohio State University. The pilot crashed outside Newcomerstown.

The NTSB report mentions that the toxicology and autopsy reports were not significant. The probable cause was listed as loss of control during an attempt to deal with an electrical issue. The toxicology report notes that the pilot was on blood pressure and cholesterol medications. The autopsy report is not in the docket. This is disappointing. Was the gentleman overweight? Was his heart enlarged? Had he had previous surgical procedures?

ERA12FA196

This crash killed three people in Florida during a landing in a congested pattern. The ATC information wasn't fully understood by the pilot, who then overreacted to perceived traffic he felt was in near proximity.

WPR12FA067

This accident was brought on by two airplanes in close proximity under ATC direction. It appears that the Cirrus passed into the wake turbulence of a Gulfstream and was unable to recover. No clear medical issues were identified.

CEN12FA083

Four persons were killed when a non-IFR pilot who the NTSB investigator strongly hinted was not overly accurate in logging his instrument or PIC time flew into IMC conditions after apparently not checking weather prior to a cross-country flight. This is on the border, but three people were killed; improper planning? This looks like a negligent homicide. I'll call it medical. If we are using the word *probable*, it is probable that a sane, rational person would check weather, maintain currency, and not end up with three passengers in a cloud and then a graveyard.

ERA12FA068

This occurred in Boynton Beach, Florida, killing two persons. In this particular homicide, a pilot who had no clear training in acrobatics decided to kill himself and another person by performing acrobatics in an airplane for which acrobatic flight is prohibited. And this wasn't simply a one-off bad decision or a momentary lapse of judgment. He'd done it before and gotten a pass on his first attempt at cheating death. The second time wasn't a charm. This is a medical/judgment-related homicide.

Performing stunts in an aircraft not designed for stunts is pretty simple to figure out.

CEN12FA037

Speaking of homicides, ten to fifteen minutes into this flight, the airplane ran out of fuel. In fairness, the pilot did call to ask that the plane be fueled before the flight. In fairness to the deceased passenger's memory, it is the job of the pilot to preflight the aircraft. It is also important to realize that the low-fuel alert was made clear on the glass cockpit display *during taxi out to takeoff.* This was extreme negligence. In the absence of any toxicological data or medical records for the pilot, I consider this a medical issue. People always ask me why I think having your receptionist schedule your flight medicals is a bit of a red flag. Read this accident report. Flying isn't about delegating responsibility; it is about *having* responsibility.

ERA12FA030A

This Danbury, Connecticut, nighttime crash killed a private pilot when he wrecked while in the pattern. The sixty-four-year-old pilot with naproxen in his system struck a hazard tower short of the runway that was designed to warn incoming pilots of a residential neighborhood. There was no evidence that the pilot had ever landed at this particular airport previously. I take naproxen—*when* I am in pain.

CEN11FA629

IMC conditions were present in West Liberty, Ohio, as the next Cirrus accident report stated. The accident occurred on September 8, 2011, at 11:22 in the morning. The fifty-one-year-old pilot had completed his last flight review six days prior. He was not instrument rated.

The NTSB report does the heavy lifting on this accident:

An autopsy of the pilot was performed at the Montgomery County Coroner's Office in Dayton, Ohio, on September 9, 2011. The "Cause of Death" was listed as multiple blunt force injuries.

A Forensic Toxicology Fatal Accident Report was prepared by the FAA Civil Aerospace Medical Institute. The results were negative for carbon monoxide, cyanide, and ethanol. The following substances were identified in the toxicology report: 19.73 (ug/ml, ug/g) Acetaminophen detected in blood (cavity); codeine not detected in blood (cavity); 0.161 (ug/ml, ug/g) codeine detected in liver; 0.152 (ug/ml, ug/g) diazepam detected in blood (cavity); 0.458 (ug/ml, ug/g) diazepam detected in liver; dihydrocodeine detected in blood (cavity); 0.201 (ug/ml, ug/g) dihydrocodeine detected in liver; 0.46 (ug/ml, ug/g) hydrocodone detected in liver; 0.091 (ug/ml, ug/g) hydrocodone detected in blood (cavity); 0.999 (ug/ml, ug/g) nordiazepam detected in liver; 0.21 (ug/ml, ug/g) nordiazepam detected in blood (cavity); 0.219 (ug/ml, ug/g) oxazepam detected in liver; 0.43 (ug/ml, ug/g) oxazepam detected in blood (cavity); oxycodone not detected in blood (cavity); oxycodone detected in liver; temazepam detected in liver; 0.094 (ug/ml, ug/g) temazepam detected in blood (cavity); 0.7593 (ug/ml, ug/g) tetrahydrocannabinol (marijuana) detected in heart; 6.3795 (ug/ml, ug/g) tetrahydrocannabinol detected in lung; 0.0959 (ug/ml, ug/g) tetrahydrocannabinol carboxylic acid (marijuana) detected in heart; and 0.1686 (ug/ml, ug/g) tetrahydrocannabinol carboxylic acid detected in lung.

Acetaminophen is an analgesic marketed under the brand name Tylenol. It is available over the counter and by prescription in a number of combination medications. Diazepam is a Schedule IV controlled substance from the benzodiazepine class marketed under the brand name Valium. Nordiazepam is a metabolite of diazepam. Oxazepam and temazepam are psychoactive metabolites of diazepam and in addition are marketed separately as Schedule IV controlled substances under the brand names Serax and Restoril. Codeine, oxycodone, and hydrocodone are unique drugs and not metabolites of one another; all are opiate analgesics (narcotics). Codeine is a Schedule II controlled substance and is marketed in combination with acetaminophen under the brand names Tylenol #2, #3, and #4. Oxycodone is a Schedule II controlled substance and is marketed under brand names Percocet and Roxicet in combination with acetaminophen as well as OxyContin when in isolation. Hydrocodone is a Schedule III controlled substance and is marketed under the brand names Lortab, Vicodin, and Norco. Dihydrocodeine is an active metabolite of hydrocodone. Hydromorphone is an active metabolite of hydrocodone and is a Schedule II controlled substance marketed under the brand name Dilaudid.

Hard to mess it up when the FAA toxicology report hands it to you on a platter, eh? Did I mention this?

Witnesses reported that the pilot intended to land at Urbana, Ohio, located about 15 nautical miles (nm) south of EDJ and pick up a passenger. They were planning to fly to Jackson, Ohio, located about 100 nm southeast of EDJ. The passenger reported that he expected to be picked up at Urbana around 1115, but the airplane never arrived.

Lucky passenger. This was pretty clearly a medically related crash. It included the following:

- Narcotics
- Muscle relaxants
- Marijuana

Per the NTSB: "It is very likely that the pilot was impaired by drug use at the time of the accident."

Included in this accident's NTSB docket file was an NTSB medical report. Nice to know such a thing can occasionally happen. Never mind—they just regurgitated the FAA's toxicology report. No attempt was made to find out where the pilot obtained these prescription meds (and one nonprescription one). Obviously, this is important, because the prescriber would also likely have insight into other past medical records of the pilot.

The point of all this: make sure you know the truth about your pilot friends *before* you get in a $500,000 airplane with them. They may just be stoned on narcotics, pot, muscle relaxants, and sleeping aids.

Hell, I wouldn't even fly light sport with this gentleman, regardless of what a wonderful job the DMV did making sure he was safe.

WPR11FA354

This accident occurred in the Kaibab of Arizona, resulting in two deaths during VFR conditions. The airplane left South Carolina at 8:00 a.m. The flight was en route to Henderson, Nevada.

"Conditions conducive to controlled flight into terrain included fatigue due to the pilots' long duty day, the dark night light condition, the lack of ground lighting in the region, and the fact that neither pilot was instrument rated."

That seems a fair assessment.

I would consider this a medical/judgment-related accident. There is no evidence of a chronic habit of poor decision making. There were two licensed pilots, the majority of the flight was in the daylight, and one of the pilots texted that the going was slow. This adds up to a swiss cheese of decisions versus a pattern of ill behavior. Fatigue is a medical condition.

ERA11FA414

This flight resulted in two deaths. I consider that all the factors added together equal a pilot utilizing poor judgment. I would understand a differing viewpoint, however.

Decision one: the pilot verbalized to others that he wouldn't use the parachute in an emergency; he would try to land the plane.

Decision two: the pilot didn't secure the oil cap filler assembly.

Decision three: the pilot continued on the flight despite having warnings of a low oil condition on both the multifunction display and the gauges.

Decision four: the airplane stalled during the forced landing, which wouldn't have occurred if the pilot had simply deployed the ballistic parachute.

The combination of these four decisions indicate to me a mind-set that isn't compatible with safe operation of an aircraft. Although this one was a decision where I could see both sides having an argument. One could argue back at me that often accidents are simply a matter of small coincidences, events, errors, and/or malfunctions adding up to a catastrophe. That, of course, is the very description of the swiss-cheese model of accidents. At the end of the day, I simply think that this was a pilot with pathologically bad judgment, and while we can disagree, I respect your opinion, there are a lot easier accidents for me to use for examples with a lot clearer medical causatives.

CEN11FA401

This accident occurred during IMC conditions in Ohio. The instrument-rated pilot and his passenger were killed. The pilot had a sedating medication at therapeutic levels in his system. Despite no apparent attempt to obtain medical records to assess why this pilot had the need for this prescription medication, and despite it being sedating and at a therapeutic level, the NTSB felt it couldn't determine if it played a role in the crash. I'd say that until proven otherwise, the presence of a medication known to affect judgment in the blood of a pilot knowingly heading into IMC conditions that require clarity of thought is fairly strong evidence that the pilot isn't thinking very clearly. I'd call this one medical.

CEN11FA267

In this accident, a pilot crashed and was killed half a mile short of the South Bend, Indiana, runway. The conditions were gusting winds at the time. The fifty-year-old pilot with more than three hundred hours and an instrument rating had no discovered medical issues. The toxicology screening was not done, nor were any medical records mentioned in the accident docket except for one paragraph. This paragraph has a nuance to it that further buries the ostrich's head:

> Ms. Hooper was asked to advise of details on the pilot's last medical application. She indicated that the pilot had been issued a FAA third-class medical certificate on June 2, 2009, with a limitation for corrective lenses. The pilot reported on the application for that medical certificate that he had accumulated 217.8 hours of total flight time and 45.8 hours of flight in the six months prior to that application.

Do you see the feathers?

The ostrich head here is obvious, but you have to look for its footprint. The *only* way the NTSB investigated any medical issues on this pilot appears to have been a phone conversation with the FAA about the pilot's last medical certificate. An investigator asked (Ms. Hooper), who would have been an FAA employee or possibly a subcontracted employee. The NTSB didn't obtain the records, review the records, and then make a determination. It appears to have predicated its entire investigation of the pilot's past medical history upon a phone conversation.

The report in the docket relates to conversations, not to records. This is a verbal discussion. I cannot begin to explain how totally incomplete this would be as a method of obtaining records. Thankfully, I am fairly certain that you, the reader, don't need me to explain this point. But I am an overachiever, so here goes.

Why is this investigation woefully inadequate? There are at least five reasons:

1. The FAA, the NTSB, the AOPA, the EAA, the ALPA, and the government are all well aware that many pilots lie on their FAA medicals. My book *Flying under the Weather* has more than a hundred examples of such behavior. It is a lot of fun to read, but the salient point is serious: a lot of pilots lie on their medicals.
2. A phone conversation often leaves out a lot of important details that might make one look deeper.
3. The hours on the last medical are rarely accurate, and thus serve less value than the pilot's height and weight. At least with that you can see that ten years ago the pilot may have weighed 170 and eight years ago weighed 310. This gives you medically relevant points of reference from which to start.
4. From my numerous conversations on the phone with government personnel who aren't medical professionals, I can tell you the only thing I ever want is to get to the doctor and talk to her, because the other folks you will talk to in Oklahoma City at Aviation Medical Certification Division (AMCD) often have no idea what information I am asking them to provide. Further, they themselves are fully aware of this. So I can tell you firsthand that calling up the feds and asking for medical info over the phone is on average a nonstarter unless you are one-to-one discussing the information you want with a physician.
5. Besides that, it's not their job. An employee is going to do what you want exactly how it is described to him in his job description. *And it's not in his job description.*

The idea that the only records you would get from a crash are the hours on the last medical when you have a hospitalized patient who would have had a history and physical performed, whose family would have visited, and whose doctors' records in the hospital after the crash would have had several consultation reports fully looking at complicating factors is a severe sign of ignorance or incompetence, or simply a total lack of interest in investigating.

Let's look at the NTSB probable cause: "the pilot's failure to maintain airplane control while on final approach with a gusting crosswind and the subsequent aerodynamic stall and spin during the attempted go-around."

OK, the investigators mentioned a failed data logger as possibly contributing; they spent thirty-four pages looking at the mechanics. They spent one paragraph looking at the far more common cause of pilot loss of control: medical and mental fitness. One paragraph.

6

BACK INTO THE CLOUDS

ONE GLARING DIFFERENCE in the Cirrus fatal crashes versus the light-sport crashes is that there are a much larger number in the Cirrus that occur at night or in IMC conditions. This virtually doesn't happen in the light-sport class, and when it does, the crash is almost 100 percent due to a medical cause.

The importance of this paragraph is that you cannot compare IFR Cirrus crashes with VFR light-sport accidents. The platforms are vastly different. The complexity of the airplanes, the complexity of the knowledge required, the competency of the pilot, the judgment of the pilot, the attention to detail, and the level of alertness required are far more elevated in the clouds than in clear air around a local airport that you are familiar with.

When you compare daytime high-performance Cirrus fatal accidents to light-sport fatal accidents, unsurprisingly, the light-sport pilots have a far worse track record, both in numbers and in rates. So despite the Cirrus being more complex, higher performance, and so on, during daytime operations in the hands of a healthy pilot, it performs very well. Similarly, despite the far slower, far simpler nature of the light-sport class of plane, if the pilot isn't all that healthy on average, we should see higher fatal accident numbers. Of course, that is precisely what we do see.

WPR11FA021

An example of an IMC crash that killed two persons and put a Cirrus out to pasture occurred on October 21, 2010, in Agua Dulce, California, when a plane and a horse stable collided. Three horses were also killed.

The fifty-one-year-old pilot with no instrument rating had codeine in his system. There was no blood collected, and thus a true blood level wasn't obtainable. There was no further investigation into *why* this pilot with a passenger on board had codeine in his body. There is mention of an autopsy in passing. One wonders if the autopsy report was surveyed exactly like the previous accident's FAA medical exam was surveyed:

"Bob, anything on the autopsy?"

"Who are you?"

"Jim, with the NTSB."

"Never met you. Nope, the autopsy wasn't any big deal."

One can only go off what one has previously been presented with. Based on the previous fatal accident's NTSB findings, it seems far more likely than not that no one at the NTSB ever *read* the autopsy or any of this pilot's medical records. This requires investigation. Not an NTSB thorough investigation, a thorough investigation of the NTSB.

Per the NTSB:

The National Transportation Safety Board determines the probable cause(s) of this accident as follows:

The non-instrument-rated pilot's improper decision to continue the flight into instrument meteorological conditions, which resulted in spatial disorientation and loss of control.

Per the *Physician's Desk Reference* regarding codeine: "Caution against performing hazardous tasks (e.g., operating machinery/driving)."

It is sedating, and it affects judgment. Judgments such as: Should I fly into IFR?

Why is it likely this was a medically related accident? The pilot did something that demonstrated poor judgment while taking medication that impairs judgment.

WPR10FA383

Three minutes after departing a Phoenix, Arizona, airport, the pilot crashed his Cirrus next to a building. VFR conditions existed during this event.

The incident occurred during a return to the airport, so that the pilot could close the left-side cabin door, which apparently had not been secured.

The pilot was sixty-seven years of age and had almost three thousand hours, including nearly one thousand hours in the Cirrus airframe. He was instrument rated. He had more than fifty hours of flying in the past ninety days as well.

And now the rare instance: the pilot's medical records were actually obtained. Remarkably, this was because he had two antidepressants in his system, including one that is a well-known sleeping aid. So based on the toxicology report, it would seem the NTSB dug further.

This warrants discussion. In the South Bend fatal accident, there was no toxicology report done. The pilot was in the hospital prior to dying, and yet no medical records were gathered. Thus, if you connect the dots, it would appear the NTSB only goes after medical issues when the toxicology report leads it in that direction.

However, this is patently a *reactive* manner in which to perform an accident report.

In the case of mechanical issues, the NTSB is very proactive. It hires engineers; it solicits manufacturer relationships; it will tear the airplane apart looking for a cause.

In the case of the far more common human factors, it is led by the nose by a totally meaningless toxicology flowchart. The toxicology report is useful if there is something present, obviously, but equally obvious is that a negative toxicology report means absolutely nothing. After all, any physician knows about poor patient compliance. Any physician has also experienced patients with mental illnesses. These patients will often have negative toxicology reports.

Yet the NTSB evidently doesn't realize this basic concept—or worse, it understands it fully and simply wants a reason to close a case, which would be fraud, a federal crime. Knowing that a test incompletely paints a picture and then presenting a "completed" accident investigation as if it were done properly, when you yourself are fully aware that you didn't do a full exploration of causatives. What else can you call that? Even if it were done out of expediency, you have a responsibility to openly say as much.

Perhaps they should just say, "Even though we legally are allowed to obtain medical records, and even though computers make this extremely simple, and even though many of these pilots have Medicare, we simply don't really want to look too deeply into this because we like playing with engines, even though they only cause about 5 percent of fatal crashes, while pilot factors caused 95 percent." That wouldn't be fraudulent.

Let us look at the toxicology:

> Desmethylvenlafaxine (O-) detected in Liver
> .747 (ug/mL, ug/g) Desmethylvenlafaxine (O-) detected in Blood (Cavity)
>> Nortriptyline detected in Liver
4.226 (ug/ml, ug/g) Nortriptyline detected in Blood (Cavity)
>> Venlafaxine detected in Liver
>> 1.321 (ug/ml, ug/g) Venlafaxine detected in Blood (Cavity)

Nortriptyline is especially important, as it is sedating. We are now looking at a pilot flying illegally on sedating antidepressants that affect judgment, who didn't perform the very first step of the pretakeoff checklist, which, according to the NTSB report, was to secure the door.

Based on the FAA doing its job on the toxicology report, the NTSB decided in this rare case to do its job too. It obtained medical reports, which stated:

> The pilot's personal medical records reveal a history of treatment for depression, including a series of medications. From 2002 forward, the pilot was prescribed venlafaxine (marketed under the trade name Effexor) 75 mg and nortriptyline (marketed under the trade name Pamelor) 75 mg daily for his depression. Also, in 2005, the pilot underwent a sleep study that documented moderate obstructive sleep apnea. CPAP and BiPAP were tried without improvement and no clear treatment regimen was defined. He began to use a dental device and intermittently CPAP while sleeping. In March, 2009, he underwent a repeated sleep study that documented mixed obstructive and central sleep apneas that were significantly improved with CPAP. In December, 2009, his primary physician documented that he reported using his CPAP.

Dishonesty kills. To put this into real terms: the pilot lied repeatedly on his medical exams with the FAA, endangering God only knows how many people, until finally his multiple medical conditions and his lack of judgment and sociopathic illegal activities culminated in his failure to protect himself by following a simple checklist.

This investigation showed that the accident was completely medical.

Per the NTSB:

> The National Transportation Safety Board determines the probable cause(s) of this accident as follows:

The pilot's failure to maintain airspeed and airplane control during a turn from the base leg to final approach due to his diverted attention.

Well, they almost got it right.

The true *actual cause* was the pilot's decision to engage in illegal flight operations while using sedating medications and suffering from an illness he intentionally kept a secret from the monitoring agency, resulting in him lacking the judgment to not fly illegally and to fully follow a checklist.

That is my opinion; it is also pretty obvious. At the very least, it is probable.

Never forget—this accident shows that the NTSB both *can* obtain medical records and *will* occasionally do it. This also shows there is no checklist to ensure that the agency always does so. Without a flight checklist, you might land with your gear up. Accident investigations aren't a lot different, and we can prove there isn't a checklist, because the vast majority of the time the NTSB doesn't bother to get medical records. If there were a checklist to evaluate human factors, that would be one of the most basic things to put on that checklist. To omit medical records would be the very definition of *incompetence*.

ERA10FA356

In July 2010, in North Carolina, another Cirrus was destroyed. In this accident during VFR conditions, the pilot veered off the runway's surface and was killed. Two passengers were injured.

The flight was a cross-country, originating from Delaware. The sixty-six-year-old pilot had no reported medical conditions on his last FAA medical exam, per the NTSB report.

Toxicology performed was reported negative. Despite the fact that the right-side passenger suffered amputation injuries, no apparent attempt was ever made to obtain the pilot's medical records to assess what other causative issues might have been involved.

ERA10FA347

This was another flight in which, landing too fast, the pilot decided to attempt a go-around and failed. The toxicology was negative, and no other medical information was gathered.

ERA10FA259

In May 2010, two people died when yet again an airplane crashed during the landing sequence. This aircraft originated from southern Florida and was headed into Tuscaloosa, Alabama. It was the first time this pilot had tried to land at the airport in question. Apparently, an autopsy was not performed on the pilot. Toxicology was negative. The NTSB docket file is not readily accessible.

WPR10FA163

This was another cross-country trip that resulted in the death of a pilot flying on an unapproved sedating medication. This medication, whose main purpose is in treating depression, was, *per the pilot's family*, being used off-label for sleep. Presuming the family members weren't prescribing this medication to the pilot, one would assume that a physician had done so. However, no serious attempt to locate this physician's records was attempted.

The probable-cause panel findings were that the accident was mechanical. In fact, the accident would never have occurred if the pilot hadn't flown while on an unapproved medication. We will never know whether a pilot who wasn't on a sedating medicine would have had the prescience to pull the emergency parachute or to land the plane safely, but we do know for a fact that a pilot who had no business flying that day did so and died.

> The National Transportation Safety Board determines the probable cause(s) of this accident as follows: The failure of maintenance personnel to properly secure a fitting cap on the throttle and metering assembly inlet after conducting a fuel system pressure check, which resulted in a loss of engine power due to fuel starvation. Contributing to the accident was the decision by the Director of Maintenance to return the airplane to service without verifying with the assigned inspector that all annual inspection items had been completed.

CEN10FA115B

The last fatal Cirrus accident we will look at in this book occurred in February 2010, when a midair collision with a Piper aircraft engaged in glider towing resulted in three deaths, two of them in the Cirrus.

The glider pilot noticed the Cirrus just before impact and was able to pull the tow release, likely saving the lives of his two passengers, who were celebrating a birthday. There were no listed medical causes to this collision.

CONCLUSIONS FROM CIRRUS ACCIDENTS

In summation, this study of Cirrus accidents is elucidative. It demonstrates that a large number of Cirrus accidents are probably medical, and that for many others we simply lack information. In fact, You could argue that up to 40 percent of all Cirrus fatal accidents in this survey as medically related.

More important, the study points out a glaring flaw in the way accident investigation is done. For a further exploration of this, we need to know a little more about the process of an accident investigation.

For now, let us dig into the light-sport fatal accidents.

7

A LIGHTER SHADE OF FUNERAL SHROUD

IN SEPTEMBER 2004 the light-sport class came into being, with the idea that it would open up avenues for new pilots to enter aviation at a cheaper price point. In actuality, this was never the real intent. The real intent of the light-sport class was to bypass medical examinations and thus allow extremely sick or mentally ill pilots to fly without any medical oversight. There are those who might argue this statement. But when you look at their agenda, you realize that they don't even pretend the light-sport class has any real purpose except to gloss over the severe illnesses of many pilots who have no business flying.

DEN05FA100

In fact, the first fatality of the light-sport aircraft class occurred in 2005, when a billionaire, who worked on his own airplanes, wrecked because he hadn't assembled his plane properly. This happened despite his track record of being very forgetful regarding tools; he apparently left an inspection mirror in the aircraft, causing the NTSB to do a lot of unnecessary testing on this inspection mirror. The reasoning was that perhaps it had impinged on the flight controls, but this was found to be a red herring. I propose we update the term *red herring* to *bent mirror*, since the

NTSB published a lot more information about this errant mirror than the net sum of all text I have ever read about red herrings. Anyway, after chasing the bent mirror as causative, the NTSB specifically appears *not* to have looked into the pilot's medical past whatsoever.

However, when we research the NTSB files, we do have some clues as to his mind-set. Bullet points from the accident:

- The pilot/owner "meant" to register the experimental aircraft with the FAA but never got around to it. It had forty-five hours logged on it, so this wasn't because he had just started flying it.
- "The elevator trim tab was not installed (according to friends of the pilot, the pilot removed the trim tab while transporting the airplane via truck after an incident in Nebraska)."
- Blood specimens for toxicological tests were taken from the pilot by the medical examiner. According to the autopsy, the cause of death was blunt-force trauma. No other medical records were obtained.
- "During one flight, the pilot left a cordless drill on the top of the engine prior to takeoff. During the flight, the cordless drill fell off the engine and contacted the composite propeller."
- During takeoff from another airport, a piece of luggage reportedly fell from the rear of the airplane. The pilot returned to the airport to retrieve the luggage.
- "According to a friend of the pilot, the pilot stated that he did not properly latch the flaps during the landing at BUB. While over the runway, with the flaps set in the full position, the flap handle disengaged, and the flaps went to the full retracted position."
- After the incident in Nebraska, the kit manufacturer and the dealer offered to personally assist the pilot in Jackson with the repairs to the airplane; however, the pilot declined the offer for on-scene assistance.
- Several of the pilot's friends assisted him during various phases of the repairs. At some point, the pilot removed the rear

floorboard, rear control stick, rear seat and restraint system, the nose-mounted heater, the fuselage cover, and the gap cover. Because the windscreen was sewn into the fuselage covering, the pilot crafted a Lexan windscreen and riveted it onto the fuselage structure. The pilot did not replace the fuselage cover, gap covers, or doors after the repairs were completed.

- The pilot's friends also reported that he had been using an inspection mirror to search for metal shavings in the rectangular cutout of the boom tube during the days preceding the accident.
- The NTSB probable cause: "The loss of airplane pitch control resulting from the pilot/owner's improper reinstallation of the rear locking collar on the elevator control torque tube, which allowed the torque tube to move rearward during flight and loosen the elevator control cable tension."

What does this tell us? Nothing completely, but it hints rather poignantly at a person who suffered from a problem with attention to detail and a need to fix things for himself and not obtain qualified help. Tragically, his decisions caused his demise. On a bright note, there was no one occupying the rear seat; he hadn't reinstalled it yet.

We do know without question that he had a primary-care doctor and medical records, and those were not investigated.

8

WHAT CONSTITUTES A MEDICAL ACCIDENT

IT IS IMPORTANT to have clear definitions to prevent misunderstandings. For example, the NTSB clearly hasn't decided to use an honest definition of *probable*. Because of this, fatal accidents that are without question medically related are misclassified. The presence of a measuring stick, a scorecard, or even basic common sense when assigning a definition of the term could fix that quite easily.

I define a medical accident as an accident wherein a person in full control of her faculties would not have demonstrated the choices that the pilot made based on the information presented. For example: a pilot who hasn't flown in twenty years decides to take up an airplane for the first time when she'd just bought it and didn't have it inspected. That is a medical accident. With that in mind, one of the most important parts of whether an accident is medical or not begins with the go or no-go decision to fly that day.

You will notice there is no mention of toxicology or autopsy in my definition. This is because a toxicology report or an autopsy report adds information only in its presence, while telling us nothing at all in its absence. Use the previous paragraph to understand my point. None of the pilot's choices are necessarily related to anything that would show on a toxicology screen.

In my definition, a 112-year-old pilot who is mentally ill and untreated might buy an aircraft under the delusion he is still twenty-six and still competent. When he wrecks and dies, an autopsy and a toxicology report might or might not be done. If the toxicology report shows the absence of drugs in the pilot's system, then it hasn't told us anything about the cause. It has only eliminated potential issues.

A toxicology report won't show you a thing about a person with delusions or dementia. An autopsy on a highly traumatized corpse often does not focus on the mental processing capability either. Thus, if the toxicology report shows a ton of cocaine in a pilot's blood or the autopsy shows the nostrils packed with a white substance, that is additive. But in the absence of this information, we still haven't investigated the pilot's health in any real, meaningful way.

We all know this intuitively, and we can read almost weekly stories about police officers facing off with mentally ill patients who are off their medications. Their toxicology and autopsy reports may show bullet wounds but would show zero direct evidence of mental instability. They were off their medications. That can happen with pilots quite easily as well. Their medical and psychiatric records can fill file cabinets, but the autopsy and toxicology would be negative.

One of the most common answers I get when I examine a pilot over age sixty is, "I don't really have one."

The question I asked them: "Who is your regular doctor?"

DEN05FA101

According to several witnesses in the area, the pilot had been attempting to land to the west on a grass strip, just north of Marble, Colorado. The pilot had made approximately *five attempts* to land prior to the accident. During the sixth approach, the airplane touched down approximately midfield, the pilot added power and the airplane became airborne again. Witnesses stated that the airplane struck a road embankment at the end of the runway, continued in a steep climb, and then struck several 60-foot-high aspen trees approximately 150 feet west of the end of the runway. The airplane "rolled off hard to the right," and impacted the southbound lane of County Road 3 in a nose low attitude.

Already this sounds ominous.

The pilot, age 76, held a private pilot certificate with airplane single-engine land privileges. This certificate was issued on October 16, 1990. The pilot had been issued a third-class airman medical certificate on December 20, 2002. The certificate contained the limitations "Must wear corrective lenses for near and distant vision" and "Not valid for any class after December 21, 2004."

He therefore had a known medical condition. How do I know he had a known medical condition? In 2004 the FAA placed him on a restricted certificate. The reasons the FAA did this and the medical reports regarding this pilot were stored by the FAA. It would be easy for the NTSB to get them; an investigator could simply call and ask the FAA to fax them over. But the NTSB made zero attempt at explaining why the pilot had previously been on a special issuance from the FAA.

The autopsy was performed in Montrose, Colorado, on July 1, 2005, as authorized by the Gunnison County Coroner's Office. The autopsy revealed no evidence of physical incapacitation or impairment that would have been causal to the accident.

Is this a true statement? Well, sort of. An autopsy isn't designed to assess mental impairment, nor can it describe physical incapacitation. You could have said that the beauty salon that the funeral procession drove by on the way to the grave didn't reveal evidence of impairment with equal accuracy.

Probable cause:

> The National Transportation Safety Board determines the probable cause(s) of this accident as follows: the pilot's improper decision to perform a go-around, and failure to maintain clearance from terrain and obstacles during a go-around. Factors contributing to the accident include the pilot's lack of recency of experience and lack of mountain flying experience, and the trees.

This accident shows what happens when a person's arrogance and lack of judgment overcome his competency. It is a medically related crash until proven otherwise. The NTSB probable cause states as much, while trying to studiously avoid stating as much.

Notice the NTSB was told he had a preexisting condition—without question—and the NTSB didn't present this to the public. It raises the question of whether the NTSB cared. If it knew why the pilot was on a special issuance, it certainly didn't bother to state what that reason was. In medicine we have a saying: "If it isn't written, it wasn't done." I am pretty confident that the NTSB didn't bother to find out.

ATL05LA140

In this accident in South Carolina, two persons were killed. The NTSB didn't bother to travel to the accident site, relying on FAA personnel to do the accident investigation instead. Ironically, it pointed several fingers at the FAA for not properly ensuring all certification standards were met by the aircraft manufacturer. Simultaneously, it trusted the FAA to investigate the two-fatality accident and expected the FAA to perform the bulk of the mission Congress tasked the NTSB with performing. You can't make this stuff up. It delegated most of the accident investigation to the same organization it found didn't perform its job as part of the probable-cause report.

To wit:

> The manufacturer of the airplane, the distributor of the airplane, and the FAA inspector who issued the airworthiness certificate for the airplane did not ensure that all items required by the ASTM Consensus Standards for LSA airplanes were included in the Pilot Operating Handbook during the airplane certification process. (Information was omitted for regarding fuel capacity, service ceiling, best angle and rate of climb, short field takeoff and landing, balked landing, and towing/tie-down). FAA Order 8130.2F, Airworthiness Certification of Aircraft and Related Products, Change 1, dated April 1, 2005, did not contain any information pertaining to the Consensus Standards or Maintenance Quality Assurance System. There were no written procedures or guidance in FAA Order 8130.2F for FAA inspectors regarding the required items that are included in the Statement of Compliance. No evidence was found to indicate that the findings regarding the Consensus Standards were related to this accident. In its final review of the "Certification of Aircraft and Airmen for the Operation of Light-Sport Aircraft," the FAA stated: "The FAA believes that the manufacturer's statement of compliance is appropriate for determining whether a light-sport aircraft meets consensus standards."

Evidently, farming out your own job isn't just the bailiwick of the NTSB. The humor of this situation is that the NTSB farms out the mass of its accident investigation to the FAA—while blaming it for not doing its job. That takes a lot of gall. You farm out *your* responsibility to an organization, and then while it tries to do your job and its own job, you criticize it for not doing its job, while it is trying to do your job for you. You can't make this stuff up.

If you think the FAA isn't doing their job, shouldn't you do your job instead of asking them to do it? After all, you don't think they can do their job—would you logically think they could do yours?

The fact that the NTSB is correct and that it is a bit interesting that the FAA would believe a manufacturer's statement of compliance is a totally separate issue outside the scope of this book.

Additionally, if you are going to farm out an investigation of an accident that 95 percent of the time will have human causative factors, perhaps a well-thought-out checklist for these investigations would include all the items needed to assess these human factors handed to the people to whom you are relegating the investigatory process. If you aren't happy with their performance of their job, you might want to be pretty explicit in how you would like them to do yours.

LAX06LA105

In this accident, little medical information is available. The aircraft wing collapsed, leading to two deaths. We'll consider this one nonmedical for the time being, until we have some other evidence.

NYC06LA171

This fatal accident was clearly medical. It was death by extremely faulty synapses in the region of the brain that determines judgment. In this accident, a gentleman with no aviation experience decided to learn to fly by having a friend who wasn't an instructor advise him. His friend stayed on the ground and used a radio to communicate with him. It didn't go well, primarily because the gentleman evidently had as much experience installing the parachute as he did flying this airplane: none.

Now, hypothetically, would a negative toxicology report make this a nonmedical exam? There isn't a toxicology report for being on the tail end of the decision-making bell curve. The answer is no.

Ask yourself this about this accident. If the pilot is also the mechanic who installed the parachute, as in this accident, how much more important is it to assess the pilot/mechanic's physical and mental health, including his judgment, level of fatigue, and eyesight?

CHI06FA224

In this accident, a pilot who wasn't comfortable flying alone in his aircraft found a person to fly home with him from an event. During this time period, they evidently didn't firmly attach the fuel cap, causing fuel exhaustion. They then flew out over water as they returned to the pilot's destination, but they didn't stay within glide range of land. The pilot drowned after ignoring the fuel-status warnings, taking them as being in error. The fact that the pilot couldn't swim gives you a bit of insight as well.

The NTSB considered the passenger as the pilot in command (PIC) in this flight, when evidently he was just along as a safety pilot, which is curious until one finds that the pilot wasn't current in his proficiency training. There are many aspects to the various stories given in the narrative that cloud the issue. The passenger appears to have been considered by the NTSB to be the only competent pilot on board. Besides not explaining this logic, they additionally do not explore in detail the pilot's medical history.

MIA06LA135

Fatigue and insulin-controlled diabetes clearly played roles in this accident. The pilot crashed after taking off from a private airport he had landed on without permission.

The presence of antidepressants doesn't appear to have bothered the personnel who performed the limited investigation into this aviation fatality. In the case number, *MIA* means "Miami," and *LA* means "limited accident investigation." It is highly unlikely the NTSB bothered to even send out an investigator. The pilot's daughter was also killed during this accident. The NTSB probable-cause finding was the pilot's failure to maintain airspeed during initial climb.

The medical records apparently weren't considered important in this person with an insulin pump and antidepressants. This was pretty clearly a medical accident. Fatigue is also not going to appear on a toxicology report.

A passenger died. A pilot had two medical issues, and fatigue was also highly probable. Any investigation done appropriately into why this crash occurred would have dug into these factors.

LAX07FA026

In this accident, the light-sport aircraft class as a creation for a sick pilot to kill himself and a family member comes fully into focus. This seventy-nine-year-old was previously under a special issuance for moderate to severe coronary-artery disease. He allowed this medical to lapse and, together with his son, bought a light-sport aircraft. His son did some of the mechanical work on the aircraft.

The NTSB report stated:

> The pilot's son reported to the Safety Board investigator that he was aware some of the maintenance he performed on the airplane as a private pilot-owner (prior to his being repairman-certified), was permissible under the Federal Aviation Regulations. However, he was also aware that some of the maintenance he had performed was not permissible, and it had not been recorded in the airplane's maintenance records.

Here we have two factors:

1. An elderly pilot with severe coronary-artery disease who lets his FAA medical lapse so he can "legally" fly light sport with less medical oversight.
2. A son doing illegal maintenance on his airplane. The father lacked either the judgment, the common sense, or the sanity to feel this might be an issue.

NTSB further stated:

> The pilot's family reported that the probable weight of the pilot and passenger was 375 pounds. The Safety Board investigator estimated 7 pounds of baggage was on board. AMD estimated that, based upon 10 pounds of fuel burning off since takeoff, the fuel weight was 170 pounds. The airplane's empty weight was 836 pounds. In total, the airplane weighed about 1,388 pounds at the time of the accident.
>
> This is about 68 pounds over the maximum authorized gross weight of 1,320 pounds. The airplane's calculated center of gravity was 15.264 inches aft of datum, near the center of the balance envelope.

This is a third slice of swiss cheese: the pilot overloads the airplane, indicating a degree of carelessness.

NTSB continued, "The FAA's Civil Aerospace Medical Institute (CAMI), Oklahoma City, Oklahoma, performed forensic toxicology on specimens from the pilot. No ethanol or drugs of abuse were detected."

And they also noted:

> According to the airplane's FAA "Operating Limitations: Light Sport Aircraft" form issued July 20, 2006, noncompliance with the limitations "...will render the airworthiness certificate invalid..." and "any change, alteration, or repair not in accordance with the manufacturer's instructions and approval will render the airworthiness certificate invalid..." Also, any maintenance must be recorded in the aircraft's maintenance records."

Thus, this aircraft wasn't legal to fly. Therefore, the seventy-nine-year-old pilot's wife, who was killed in the accident, was a victim of a homicide.

Of interest also is what the toxicology report left out: What *legal* medications was the pilot taking? This seems a bit important. The toxicology report carefully states no ethanol or drugs of abuse were detected. It does not make any mention of legally prescribed drugs in a seventy-nine-year-old with known severe medical issues. Is this intentional? Does the NTSB want us to not know what meds the pilot was legally taking? Did anyone even bother to test for legal drugs? Did the pilot not have good cardiology follow-up, and was he refusing to take his medications? Did he have memory loss and forget to take them?

What kind of insurance do most seventy-nine-year-olds carry? Five faxed medical records release forms to Medicare, VA, and the three largest insurance carriers in Fair Oaks, California, would have likely told us a lot more information. It would have taken about five extra minutes. It is almost like not properly preflighting an aircraft. In today's auto-filled, auto-faxed world, the cost: nothing.

9

THE CRIMINALS

NYC07FA025

IN THIS ACCIDENT, a pilot flying illegally after lying on the FAA medical exam form and possibly coercing a medical professional to also lie for him ran out of gas, altitude, and life when he took up an airplane with practically no fuel in the tank and promptly crashed.

The fact that he was a flight instructor seems important as well. Sadly, the NTSB apparently didn't go back and look for any medical records to assess whether the pilot had actually ever stopped taking antidepressants.

Originally, his exam was deferred because he was on two anti-depressants. Then he submitted a letter from a doctor stating that he was now off all medications (that he had been on "for years") and was fine. The FAA allowed him a medical, after which he had a subsequent FAA medical a couple of years later and lied about his mental-health history. One of the same antidepressants he claimed to have stopped taking came up in his toxicology report. Based on the information given, this was a criminal and a medical fatal accident. The FAA tells pilots that they must ground themselves if they resume antidepressants.

CEN12FA073

In this accident, a sixty-nine-year-old who legally was not allowed to solo, being only a student who hadn't been signed off on yet, did so anyway. He died on his second flight in the airframe type. His instructor stated that on the first flight, the student hadn't landed or taken off in the craft. Mental faculties certainly would be in question. Let's look at the toxicology and see if he was on or off his medications:

> Pseudoephedrine is a non-sedating over-the-counter decongestant found in various cold and allergy medications. Chlorpheniramine is a sedating antihistamine used to treat allergy and common cold symptoms. It is available over the counter under various trade names including Chlor-Trimeton and Chlortabs. Chlorpheniramine caries the warning—"may impair mental and/or physical ability required for the performance of potentially hazardous tasks (e.g., driving, operating heavy machinery)."

I would love to also see his other medical records, as well as his psychiatric ones. But suffice it to say: when you are taking a sedative, it is a sign of mental illness to fly your aircraft by yourself, illegally, for the first time ever.

DEN07FA136

In this accident, a fifty-seven-year-old pilot took a passenger to his death in an aircraft that hadn't been given an annual inspection within the past twelve months and that had improperly labeled speed arcs on the airspeed indicator. He had a total of five or six hours in the airplane before he took a passenger to his death. Taking people up in an airplane that doesn't meet standards would be considered a sociopathic act by most normal persons. This was a medically caused crash. Lack of judgment is a medical condition.

LAX08LA024

In this flight, a pilot illegally operated a light-sport aircraft at night. The fifty-four-year-old hadn't had a medical for eight years and couldn't legally fly at night, as the aircraft wasn't certified by the FAA for night operations. I almost forgot this detail: he had marijuana in his blood. The aircraft broke apart in flight because its cables weren't properly installed. You want to be on your A game when you take up an illegal aircraft for an illegal flight. This was definitively a medical fatality. You won't find that clearly spelled out in the NTSB probable-cause report. I'll do it for them here. Flying illegally is a sign of mental aberrancy.

CHI08LA031

I'll let you read another NTSB excerpt:

> According to Federal Aviation Administration (FAA) records, the pilot of N634WB, age 71, held a private pilot certificate with an airplane single-engine land rating. He was not instrument rated. The pilot's last aviation medical examination was completed on August 4, 1994, when he was issued a third-class medical certificate with no limitations or restrictions. The pilot's flight logbook indicated that he had accumulated 119.2 hours' total flight time, of which 80.7 hours were as pilot-in-command. He had accumulated 3.5 hours at night and 3.6 hours in simulated instrument conditions. The pilot did not have any flight experience in a model 601 XL airplane before the accident flight. The pilot's most current flight review, as required by 14 CFR Part 61.56, was completed on September 1, 1991. The last documented flight was completed on September 1, 1998, for a conventional landing gear orientation flight with a flight instructor. According to the pilot's wife, it had been nearly 10 years since he last piloted an aircraft.

This one isn't difficult.

This gentleman bought an airplane, took it up on its very first flight without apparently bothering to get any instruction, and killed himself. The total lack of common sense involved makes one wonder what his geriatrician found on the gentleman's last mental-health evaluation. The NTSB apparently wasn't all that curious; it didn't look. It did mention that he was on two medications useful for treating hypertension as well as heart disease.

NYC08LA087

In this flight, a pilot who wasn't licensed as a sport pilot took up an amateur-built airplane that wasn't certified, after previously doing it and being told by his flight instructor, who was also the person who would have examined the airworthiness of the airplane, not to take the airplane up until it passed inspection. The pilot ignored this, and the pilot died. This would be a medical fatality.

ERA11LA496

This was another illegal flight. A pilot who had not passed his last FAA medical and thus couldn't legally fly light sport went flying and is believed to have suffered a fatal heart attack or arrhythmia per the autopsy. It is possible that either his lymphoma or his lymphoma therapy killed him. I'm not sure if he was getting any therapy, though; the accident investigation was done by the NTSB, so we don't see that type of information. His diabetes could have also been an issue or his diabetes medication. In any event, we know he died after flying when he had not passed his last FAA medical.

One could actually quibble on this point, since to the best of my knowledge, there is no situation legally for a person to be allowed to fly light sport when he has had his last medical exam deferred but while it was four months into the review process. My mind says, you didn't pass your last medical, ergo, you can't fly. A lawyer might say, "He also didn't fail it…yet."

The FAA certainly had his doctors' names, his medical reports, and so on. I could have had his medical records within a week with three simple faxes to his primary-care office, his insurance carrier, and his oncologist. But again, I find this type of information regarding a pilot who purportedly died owing to a medical cause important.

If I were an accident investigator and I found out that five months prior to the accident, a pilot had reported his doctor visits to an FAA medical examiner, I'd put my feet up on the desk, thinking about how easy it was going to be to get this gentleman's history. NTSB, not so much. It requires *wanting* to investigate an accident to actually investigate an accident.

Read this:

> The pilot, age sixty-three, held a private pilot certificate, with ratings for airplane single-engine land, airplane multiengine land, and instrument airplane. He also held an LSA repairman certificate. The pilot's most recent FAA third-class medical certificate was issued on October 27, 2003. The pilot applied for another third-class medical certificate on May 9, 2011; however, the medical application was deferred for review due to a history of coronary artery disease, hypertension, lymphoma, and diabetes.

Now consider this:

1. The only way the FAA would know he had these diseases is if the pilot told the aviation medical examiner.
2. The FAA will deny a medical if they do not receive medical records to review.
3. The medical happened May 9, the accident September 21, over four months later.

4. The FAA either had his medical records or the names of his doctors, or the pilot refused to provide this information or hadn't bothered.
5. Either way, the easiest thing in the world would be to do exactly what the NTSB has done sporadically in other accidents: obtain the complete FAA records for this pilot.
6. It didn't.

The autopsy report led them to "heart attack." In fairness, that is rarely the case, and you need a protocol in place to get a pilot's medical records postaccident. They do not have such a protocol.

Another point, given how many of these accidents have shown evidence of illegal activity, we should all agree that when a passenger is killed, there is a definitive possibility that these should be homicide investigations until proven otherwise. The NTSB apparently doesn't grasp this point.

CEN13LA063

This accident was another case of criminal action. The pilot wasn't legally allowed to pilot a light-sport aircraft, as his last FAA medical examination was denied because of coronary-artery disease. This gentleman took his first and last flight in an aircraft he'd just purchased.

The pilot additionally had diphenhydramine in his system at a low level and was also taking medication associated with arrhythmia treatment.

"The cause of death was determined to be from multiple injuries."

No other medical records were obtained. The autopsy did show atherosclerotic heart disease, as well as evidence of a previous heart attack.

CEN13FA338

This one wasn't overly difficult. A pilot flying illegally, after being denied a medical by the FAA, took another pilot on a night cross-country flight in a light-sport aircraft.

This is an interesting flight, however, for several reasons:

1. The aircraft manufacturer probably sent out an incorrect fuel placard, causing the pilots to overestimate the fuel load.
2. The criminal pilot didn't provide an adequate reserve, even if he had been able to calculate the usable fuel.
3. The aircraft wasn't approved for night flight.

The NTSB probable-cause report again downplays the possibility of the pilot's medical condition playing a role in the accident, despite the pilot making several terrible judgment calls:

> The ATP had severe heart disease, hypertension, and a history of stroke, which increased his risk for a cardiac arrhythmia; however, the autopsy found no evidence of a recent heart attack. The ATP also had a history of depression, and toxicological tests were positive for therapeutic levels of the antidepressant medication citalopram, which has an acceptable side effect profile. It could not be determined if the pilot was impaired by cardiac symptoms or depression around the time of the accident; however, the circumstances of the accident make it unlikely.

Now, that is quite amusing. The NTSB is claiming that the circumstances of the accident make it unlikely his medical issues were impairing him. He didn't properly plan the fuel. He knowingly chose to fly illegally. He didn't properly plan the flight so that it occurred in daytime hours.

This seems to me to be an impaired thought process—the type of thought process one would see in a fatalistic, depressed patient who isn't getting a lot of oxygen to his brain or who has suffered some sort of brain injury affecting his judgment, like, say, oh, I don't know, a stroke or two.

The idea that the circumstances aren't indicative of an impaired pilot flies in the face of the facts. The circumstances prove almost unequivocally that the pilot was suffering from a mental impairment. Last I heard, strokes affect the brain, as does depression and severe heart disease. I almost liked it better when the NTSB didn't say anything at all and didn't get medical records. Now it is talking gibberish.

Interestingly, the NTSB report states that the pilot had no evidence of a recent heart attack. Yet his wife was interviewed (NTSB docket), and she stated he had had heart surgery less than three months previously. Finding those hospital records would have most likely been extremely easy to do. It wasn't done.

It is almost as if the NTSB doesn't believe that *thinking* and *decision making* are part of the human mind. Which means its hiring process must be incredible. After all, if it doesn't consider thinking and decision making integral to flying safely and doesn't realize it is part of the brain, how is the NTSB able to vet applicants for employment?

Let's pile on a little more. Antidepressants are known for not working right away, so while the blood level may have been therapeutic, the NTSB investigator shows a glaring lack of knowledge regarding how these medications work. Additionally, being at a laboratory level deemed "therapeutic" is meaningless if the medication isn't working. To know that would require *records*, since if being therapeutic simply by looking at blood levels was equivalent to being efficacious, there would be no real need for ever changing a person from one antidepressant to another.

If the investigator were serious about finding out whether the pilot was impaired by his depression, perhaps obtaining his records via subpoena would have been appropriate. Instead, the investigator showed the world that he didn't care enough to bother with it. Unless, of course, a deeper issue exists: the NTSB management prevents investigators from doing full accident investigations.

WPR14FA135

In this accident, a pilot who was flying tours illegally did some jury-rigging on his airplane and ended up making an illegal flight a deadly one. He and the person going on the tour were both killed. The pilot was legally able to work on his plane, as he had a light-sport repairman certificate; however, the end result is that perhaps that rule should be revisited at some point. An innocent tourist died in this "introductory flight training" event. The NTSB reports that none of the "students" on these "introductory flight training" events ever seemed to do follow-up training. It also reported that the FAA was aware that this illegal activity was occurring but had limited resources to stop the practice. This seems a bit of a punt. But the purpose of the book isn't to expose tourists to the illegal practices of pilots in Hawaii, so we will move on.

A note to the FAA: anytime you are aware of any illegal activity you are resource limited to investigate, it would be a good idea to send a direct note to the NTSB, so it can say, "The FAA and the NSTB were aware that illegal activity…" The concrete can be wet and cold under a bus, and misery loves company. If the NTSB wants to throw you under the bus, invite it along as well.

You might also point out to them the following: if limited resources prevent the FAA from doing its job, and if the NTSB farms out the vast majority of its investigative work to the FAA, then the NTSB should be well aware that the FAA isn't going to do the NTSB's job very well, given that it lacks the resources to do its own job.

The NTSB, if we are to believe its accident reports, is stating that the entire process of accident reports is just a farce because of the fact that these accidents are knowingly farmed out to people the NTSB is well aware lack the resources to adequately fulfill their own mandates.

10

THE SICK

LAX07LA032

THIS ACCIDENT KILLED a student pilot with an undisclosed issue, most likely a physical limitation based on the fact that one year previously he had been given a limited medical that restricted him to student pilot privileges only. This is a hint that he may have needed a medical flight test because of a fixed defect, such as monocular vision, amputation, and so on.

I can't be certain, because the government organization tasked with investigating accidents left off this fairly important detail, leaving a void in the investigation that a light-sport aircraft could fly through. The student pilot was with a passenger who was also a private pilot, and there were no witnesses to the actual event, although a person on the ground did hear the sounds of the aircraft just prior to the crash.

The passenger additionally had some type of medical issue that the NTSB had zero interest in explaining. Here are the narrative excerpts from the reports that show the NTSB knew of an issue, raised the issue, and then simply put the issue back into the closet without explaining the issue.

Pilot 1
An examination of the pilot's personal logbook indicated that he had taken, and passed satisfactorily, the sport pilot practical test

on October 8, 2006. He had been issued a third-class medical certificate on February 22, 2005. The following restrictions were noted on his medical certificate: must wear corrective lenses for near and distant vision; valid for student pilot purposes only; not valid for any class after.

According to the pilot's logbook he had an estimated total flight time of 270 hours. He logged an estimated twelve hours in the last ninety days. His personal logbook recorded no flight hours in the last thirty days. He had an estimated 130 hours in the accident make and model.

Pilot 2

A review of the FAA airman records revealed the pilot held a private pilot certificate with an airplane single engine land and instrument airplane ratings. At the time of the accident, the pilot's medical certificate was pending, with March 16, 2006, as the medical date. On his last medical application, the pilot reported a total time of 770 hours.

Let's review. The student pilot likely had a fixed medical defect (and probably another separate health issue) that would have required a medical flight test prior to legally flying, since his medical stated, "not valid for any class after his student medical expired." That is the legal speak that occurs on medical certificates that indicates the presence of a medical issue. A student pilot certificate on a pilot with no medical issues would say, "limitations: NONE." Having a fixed defect, the certificate should read, "Valid for student pilot privileges only." Having both a medical issue and possibly an additional fixed issue, the certificate should read, "Valid for student pilot privileges only. Not valid for any class after."

The other alternative that could explain the medical certificate limitations is that the FAA doctor simply typed in the wrong limitation. That used to happen an awful lot because the certificates in that 2006 timeframe were almost always typed on typewriters. With three-thousand-plus flight examiners, you'd often have variations on a theme. Now, with computerized drop-down lists, it has been a lot more consistent. It's as if now, with a checklist, we flight doctors make a lot fewer mistakes.

In any event, this points out why the NTSB needs to get records, not just ask the FAA over the phone what was typed on the last certificate. It is the difference between investigating and ignoring an issue.

In March of that year, the passenger sent medical records or an exam to the FAA that required further review, owing to a medical condition. That is what "medical certificate was pending" means. The normal process is to do the medical on day one and issue the certificate on day one. It is only when a pilot has a medical condition that you would likely see "medical certificate pending."

So what were the issues? Well, that would require an accident investigation, so let's sit back and wait, perhaps hold our breath as well. This accident narrative is disgraceful. The investigator openly hints at two medical problems and then doesn't explain how these problems didn't contribute to the crash.

That is a disservice to the taxpayer, as well as the families of the pilots. If the one pilot was color-blind and the other had passed a kidney stone in February with excellent follow-up, and if the NTSB had simply explained this, I would have absolutely nothing to say. Raising the suspicion of an issue and then not fully explaining how the issue is a "bent mirror" is simply wrong.

This accident needs more information.

NYC08LA165

I call this the "silver platter" accident.

The pilot was flying illegally on several medications that would have prevented him from legally operating an aircraft. He was performing aerial application, a commercial venture, and thus would be required to have a current second-class medical, which he didn't. The fact that he was flying a light-sport aircraft he had fitted to apply chemicals is a "bent mirror."

The sixty-seven-year-old dishonest criminal had quite a few medical issues.

Per the NTSB:

The Henry County Medical Examiner, Tennessee Department of Health and Environment, conducted an autopsy on the pilot. The cause of death was cited as "multiple blunt force injuries." The medical examiner's report noted that the pilot had a "history of diabetes and a cardiac history of unknown etiology, an enlarged heart, severe coronary artery disease, and gallstones." Toxicological testing of the pilot's tissue samples was conducted by the FAA Civil Aero Medical Institute, and gabapentin, varenicline, and atenolol were detected.

The pilot's most recent application for 2nd class Airman Medical Certificate, dated 12/27/2006, noted "No" to "Do You Currently Use Any Medication," and to all conditions under "Medical History," including specifically "Heart or Vascular Problems," "Diabetes," "Neurological disorders," and "Mental disorders of any sort; depression, anxiety, etc."

That is a minimum of four medically grounding conditions:

1. Chantix usage (varenicline)
2. Gabapentin usage
3. Heart disease
4. Diabetes

Also in the probable-cause report we see a chillingly ironic admission: "He did not note any medications or medical conditions on his most recent application for medical certificate, but it is possible that the medications were initially prescribed since that application."

The NTSB investigator is admitting, "This pilot was taking medication that may or may not have been new, and I didn't bother to dig deeper to find out if that was the case." The NTSB investigator is openly admitting to not doing his job thoroughly.

Legally, as we find later in the book, the NTSB has full authority to obtain any and all medical records. This NTSB investigator opened Pandora's box, and despite making the astute observation that the pilot may have just started the illegal medications that would have grounded him, didn't bother to ask the next question: How many doctors *are* there in Paris, Tennessee, population ten thousand?

I am going to guess not many. There are likely even fewer pharmacies and a relatively low number of gabapentin prescriptions.

A medical professional would also ask what the coroner meant by a history of diabetes. What evidence of this was there? Were there insulin injection marks? Was there an implanted insulin pump? What knowledge did the coroner have that prompted this finding? Perhaps the coroner asked the doctor, because the NTSB certainly didn't. The investigator pretty much stated he or she didn't.

I am not sure about the reader, but if someone asked me to mention every pharmacy in America, I couldn't do it. But I can mention: CVS, Walgreens, and Google. Paris, Tennessee, has about seven pharmacies. The closest one to the pilot was Perkins. He was on multiple medications that would have required refills. You check the VA and you check Perkins pharmacy first. From there you expand your search. Find the pharmacy, you find the doctor; find the doctor, you find the records. This is kindergarten stuff here. Having to explain it is demeaning to both the author and the reader. We all know how to get information: it is simply a matter of strategy, procedure, and caring enough to do your job. A checklist might help.

Humans are mammals. Mammals have territories. Humans are creatures of habit. A human doesn't like to pass a pharmacy regularly that is five miles from his house to go to one that is six miles from his house unless there are other reasons.

But occasionally, even if you don't like the pharmacy, you are going to go to the closest one. When you do, the pharmacy will mark your doctor's name on your bottle, unless you get every single one of your medications in the mail every single time. And that is why you get Medicare and VA records when you start your investigation.

NYC08LA235

In this accident, the plane pitched up during takeoff and then crashed. There was no significant attempt made to assess pilot factors. The NTSB did mention that he was on a blood pressure medication, but no other issues were looked at seriously to determine why this pilot stalled the aircraft on takeoff.

MIA08LA164

A seventy-two-year-old pilot whose last FAA medical was three and a half years prior died when he wrecked his Ercoupe. The plane's most recent inspection was one month prior. The autopsy showed that the pilot had coronary artery disease and had had a prior heart attack. There is no report of whether the pilot knew he had heart disease.

The toxicology report mentions only ranitidine, which is taken for heartburn most commonly. But it is generally taken for a stomach type of heartburn, not very useful for a heart type of heartburn (angina). Was this pilot suffering angina and thought he only had heartburn? These are basic medical questions. Patients quite commonly miss cardiac symptoms, thinking they are not cardiac in nature. Missed heart attack symptoms are the basis for one of the most common type of lawsuit that patients win in malpractice cases.

The degree to which this pilot knew his medical conditions is totally unclear. If he did know he had heart disease, it would explain why he didn't update his medical. But then, perhaps he just didn't want to go through the hassle; after all, his Ercoupe qualified as a light-sport aircraft.

The NTSB gave us a riddle; it made no attempt to take a microscope to the pilot's health history. As a result, we are left to wonder why a pilot at age seventy-two, with a prior heart attack and scarring of his heart that would increase his risk of arrhythmias, who was taking a heartburn medicine for symptoms that might not have been heartburn, wrecked his airplane on a twelve-hundred-foot grass strip that he had landed in many times in the past. He clipped a tree during climb out. The tree was fifty feet past the runway, thirty yards to the left of it. A witness stated it looked as if the airplane had encountered a down gust, but down gusts aren't visible. What may have happened is the pilot suffered an angina attack or was distracted.

The point is that this incident wasn't truly investigated. It was given lip service. We have no idea whether this pilot should or shouldn't have been flying. For all we know, he ran a marathon the week before and did one hundred pushups daily while solving ten Sudoku puzzles a day. That is the point—without answers, we do not serve the general public in improving public safety, and we also do a disservice to the memory of the pilot. If there are passengers, then we basically slap them in the face. The fact they are dead and the family can see that we slapped them heightens the offense. The fact that the NTSB thinks no one is going to call it on this affront insults us all.

LAX08LA290

This accident paints the light-sport fiasco in a perfectly nuanced light. In this accident, a pilot who hadn't flown in about forty years decided at age seventy-four to start flying. Why? Well, we can surmise that he simply was too busy prior to this. Or we can surmise that he had major medical issues and simply couldn't have ever qualified for a medical prior to the light-sport class being invented. Let us see what the investigation tells us.

The pilot, age 74, held a private pilot certificate with a single engine land airplane rating. His last FAA medical certificate was issued in November 1970. According to the FAA inspector, who reviewed the pilot's flight logbooks, the pilot had accumulated about 265 total flight hours, with 215 of those hours acquired prior to 1968. The pilot began flying again in October 2007, receiving instruction in weight-shift aircraft with the goal of obtaining his sport pilot endorsement. In February 2008, he received about 10 hours flight instruction in a Cessna 172 and successfully completed a biennial flight review. Following the flight review, the pilot had flown about 30 hours, most of it in the accident aircraft.

This was his first day soloing and his second flight.

It is instructive that he got checked out in a 172 in February 2008. This isn't a light-sport aircraft. Was he thinking about getting a medical and decided he couldn't pass? Or was this simply a proper training platform for the pilot to get basic flight instruction? Let's dig a bit deeper.

Well, we'd like to dig deeper, but unfortunately, other than an autopsy that didn't look at existing disease and the fact his blood had two blood pressure medicines in it, the NTSB investigator evidently never stopped to consider this gentleman was likely on Medicare, likely had insurance billings identifying every major illness he had ever had in the previous nine years, never considered that Medicare is part of the US government, the same US government that employs the NTSB, and never considered that under federal law, as an investigator he had the legal right to obtain these records, as well as the legal requirement to do a full investigation such that aviation safety in the future could be improved.

What was witnessed was that the pilot took off from a touch-and-go, pulled the nose up to a steep angle, stalled the aircraft, and subsequently lost control, crashed, and died.

CHI08FA196

In this accident, a seventy-seven-year-old with high blood pressure died in the traffic pattern.

Per the NTSB: "The pilot's failure to maintain control of the airplane in the landing pattern."

Other than mentioning the toxicology report, the NTSB made no attempt to see why a seventy-seven-year-old pilot would have failed to maintain control of the airplane in the landing pattern.

CEN09LA543

In this one, a nontherapeutic level of diphenhydramine was found in the sixty-eight-year-old sport pilot's system, according to the NTSB; however, this conflicts with the FAA toxicology report, which shows no such levels. The cause of the accident was a loss of control, owing to a sharp, banking turn. No other additional data were mentioned other than a negative autopsy.

How did this happen?

It took some head-scratching, but once again, the toxicology screen on the docket was the toxicology screen for the passenger. The pilot's toxicology screen wasn't entered into the docket.

I discovered this when contacting the pathology department at Terre Haute Hospital. The sixty-eight-year-old pilot did have mild to moderate coronary-artery disease and some fatty-liver disease; however, he did not have any evidence of being treated for these conditions, as his blood didn't demonstrate medications that would be of a therapeutic nature, nor is there evidence to suggest these issues had an impact on the accident.

In a ten-minute phone call to a medical examiner, I was able to discover far more information about both the pilot's and the passenger's medical conditions than it appears the NTSB bothered to document.

In fairness, there are some states, such as Indiana, that restrict the release of autopsy reports far more than others. (In fairness to me, I mean.) Had the accident taken place in a different state, it wouldn't have taken even ten minutes of effort. Request faxed, thumbs twiddled, autopsy received. Sometimes to get answers in an investigation, you just have to actually want to get answers.

ERA10LA164

The FAA handed the next accident to the NTSB on a silver platter as well:

> MEDICAL AND PATHOLOGICAL INFORMATION
> The Office of the Medical Examiner, Georgia Bureau of Investigation, performed the autopsy on the pilot in Savannah, Georgia. The autopsy report indicated that the pilot died as a result of "blunt force injury with drowning."
>
> Other significant conditions included "arteriosclerotic cardiovascular disease" and "hypertensive heart disease."
>
> The FAA's Bioaeronautical Sciences Research Laboratory, Oklahoma City, Oklahoma, performed toxicological testing of the pilot. The testing revealed the following substances either detected or measured in both blood and urine samples:
> 112 (ug/ml, ug/g) Amitriptylene
> 0.85 (ug/ml, ug/g) Meprobamate
> 0.049 (ug/ml, ug/g) Nortriptylene
> 9.922 (ug/ml, ug/g) Tramadol

Carisoprodol
Amitriptylene and Nortriptylene were most commonly prescribed as antidepressants. Meprobamate was most commonly prescribed as an anti-anxiety medication and muscle relaxant. Carisoprodol was most commonly prescribed as a muscle relaxant. Tramadol was most commonly prescribed for relief of moderate to severe pain, often associated with arthritis.

In a telephone interview, a representative of the pilot's family revealed that the pilot's widow had no knowledge of the pilot's medical history, the physicians he may have consulted, or the point of sale for the medications he had taken. The family surmised that the pilot may have received medical treatment from the United States Department of Veterans Affairs (VA), but written and verbal requests for medical records from the VA revealed no records.

The word for this is *lazy*. The family is claiming no one knows where he got medical treatment. There is this thing called the US Mail. They deliver bills and statements to houses, including insurance information. And the widow is claiming, "Uh, I dunno." Come on.

The point here is that this family may have a very good legal reason not to want the investigator to know the truth. I guarantee you that when you have a person on a controlled substance, the NTSB can find out who the doctor is. It is part of the government. People who prescribe or fill prescriptions for controlled substances are going to be a lot more helpful than the family will. You can get the truth; you simply have to know how to do an investigation to get the truth. It starts with the controlled substance. You legally can have the sheriff go get the bottles. The bottles have the names of the physicians. The widow can't legally possess them. They are not her property, since, by law, only the pilot could be in possession of the prescribed federally controlled substance, unless he had a caregiver.

Note that I said you "can" do that. That isn't what I would do. I would simply draw a ten-mile circle around the gentleman's home and contact every pharmacy with a faxed release form. In ten minutes, the cold or flu he had a medication filled on sometime in the past six years would give you his doctor's name, and you'd then have his insurance company. This is beyond simple. It is about human nature. You have to know human nature to investigate human nature. It's integral. Going the next step isn't evidently part of the NTSB's protocol, if there even is a protocol. Not to worry—doing the least amount of work possible when you think no one is watching, that often seems to be human nature as well.

This report demonstrates that there was knowledge at the NTSB that pharmacies are places that prescribe medication. But sending out records requests to the major pharmacies to assess their databases was a bridge too far.

The NTSB found the probable cause as the following:

Post mortem examination of the pilot revealed the presence of arteriosclerotic cardiovascular disease and hypertensive heart disease, and the recent use of antidepressants, anti-anxiety, and painkilling medications. It was not known to what degree, if any, these issues affected the outcome of the flight.

The pilot's most recent medical certificate was issued nine-teen years prior to the accident, but he was not required to hold a current one while operating as a sport pilot.

The National Transportation Safety Board determines the probable cause(s) of this accident as follows:

The pilot's failure to maintain airspeed and inadvertent stall after takeoff.

Laugh or cry: flip a coin.

The probable cause of this accident was the pilot's choice to go flying while using several sedating medications and painkillers and while having severe coronary artery disease and severe pain and/or addiction, requiring said painkillers. His use of muscle relaxants while flying also probably affected his muscles required for flying. Now, really, was that so hard? The NTSB probable-cause report for this accident is simply fraud. It is ridiculous to assert that this pilot was probably not impaired. For the benefit of any NTSB personnel who might actually read this book: probable (adjective): likely to be the case or to happen.

OK, now there is truly no excuse. You have been given the definition of the word you apparently do not understand.

ERA10LA203

In this accident, we have a morbidly obese gentleman on five (that would be five) blood pressure medications, as well as diphenhydramine, who ran out of fuel. His wife, who survived the crash, stated she checked, and the tanks were full when they left. They only flew one and a half hours, and the airplane had the ability to fly six hours if properly fueled. The NTSB believed carb icing was the cause. But given the pilot's severe heart disease, his morbid obesity, and the fact that no intelligent doctor in the world would have put him on five blood pressure medications unless she had evaluated his heart and renal status, I am putting this down as caused by the pilot possibly hiding at least one medical condition from the FAA. I wager he was well aware he had heart disease, because by the time I get you on your fifth blood pressure medication, I am damn well going to have a thorough heart evaluation done on you.

The pilot's last application for airman medical certificate (third class) was dated July 16, 2007, and noted a height of 71 inches, a weight of 282 pounds, the use of propranolol, furosemide, ramipril, hydrochlorothiazide, and losartan for blood pressure control, and a blood pressure of 150/92. Postmortem examination of the pilot was performed by the Office of the Chief Medical Examiner, Forensic Sciences Center, Wilmington, Delaware. The autopsy report noted the cause of death as "multiple blunt force injuries," and documented heart size of 550 grams with 90 percent occlusion of the left anterior descending coronary artery. The pilot's spouse stated that the pilot did not snore at all. Forensic toxicology was performed on specimens of the pilot by the FAA Bioaeronautical Sciences Research Laboratory (CAMI), Oklahoma City, Oklahoma. The CAMI toxicology report was negative for ethanol, cyanide, carbon monoxide. The following drugs were detected: amlodipine in the kidney and liver, propranolol in the kidney and liver, diphenhydramine in the liver, and 0.027 ug/ml diphenhydramine in the blood.

Since I am now doing probable causes, I'd add that his morbid obesity was probably causing him such severe insomnia that he began taking antihistamines to sleep, which didn't actually address either his Pickwickian syndrome–related symptoms or his probable sleep apnea, but instead simply made him more unable to safely make good decisions. One such good decision is when to apply carb heat, or another, even more basic, is when not to fly.

In case you didn't notice, despite the five blood pressure medications, his medications weren't controlling his blood pressure. My guess is that his heart disease was very well known to his primary-care physician. I'd be curious about his renal status as well as his peripheral artery disease.

If you are really up on your medications, you have noticed the furosemide. This is an old-time blood pressure medication. Its more common use in the twenty-first century is for moderate to severe congestive heart failure.

ERA12FA107

The autopsy did the heavy lifting on this next accident, which happened on takeoff in the first flight of the airplane for several years. "The pilot's incapacitation [was] due to a ruptured berry aneurysm during takeoff."

That is actually one that an FAA medical exam probably wouldn't have caught. No medical records were gathered, so we have no idea what the FAA medical exam would have found. This was a medically caused accident, so the medical history would have been helpful.

ERA12FA395

In this accident, a sixty-four-year-old pilot with antidepressants and antidiabetic medications in his system crashed after he failed to remove the safety pin of his ballistic parachute, failed to connect the elevator properly, and failed to preflight the aircraft sufficiently.

Depression is characterized by feeling as if you are in a cloud, where making simple decisions becomes difficult and concentration is adversely impacted. I would have greatly appreciated knowing that this pilot's medical records were obtained, to see to what extent he had complained about his depression and who was treating his diabetes.

His last FAA medical examination was in 2010. If he lied on that exam, his medical was not a valid medical, and thus he was not legal to fly light sport. Passing the medical occurs only when you are honest. You don't pass it by committing a felony. That information is pertinent and should have been investigated. It was not.

I would wager that no one at the NTSB has ever considered that passing an FAA medical by dishonest means invalidates the medical and the pilot thus is flying light sport illegally. If anyone from an insurance company happens to be reading this book, you can consider that a gift. There is no reason to ever pay a criminal's insurance if they have been illegally flying light sport. Lying on a medical would automatically invalidate any insurance claim, were I elected king.

WPR12FA295

Two pilots died in a flight-review accident.

Following are some excerpts from the NTSB report:

> The pilot, age eighty-nine, held a commercial pilot certificate with an airplane single-engine land, single engine sea, and instrument airplane ratings. The most recent third class medical certificate was issued to the pilot November 3, 2005.

Hmm, now, why would anyone simply let a third-class medical lapse and go light sport? Let's read further:

According to the FAA medical case review; the 89-year-old pilot had a history of high blood pressure and coronary artery disease treated with bypass surgery and medications. He had not renewed his medical certificate since it expired November 30, 2006.

The Ventura County Medical Examiner conducted an autopsy on the pilot on July 7, 2012. The medical examiner determined that the cause of death was "...blunt force injuries." The autopsy noted a palpable subcutaneous pacemaker. The pacemaker was not interrogated. The cardiovascular system examination was limited by the degree of injury; the heart was not intact. The coronary arteries were not examined. The brain was not examined.

The FAA's Civil Aeromedical Institute (CAMI) in Oklahoma City, Oklahoma, performed toxicology tests on the pilot. According to CAMI's report, no carbon monoxide was detected in the blood and no ethanol was detected in the vitreous. Metoprolol and Valsartan were detected in the blood and urine. Ticlopidine was detected in the urine but not the blood. Metoprolol is a beta-blocker used to treat patients with cardiovascular disease. Valsartan is an angiotensin receptor blocker used to treat high blood pressure. Ticlopidine is used to prevent platelet aggregation (clotting) in patients at risk for strokes and also in people with coronary artery stents.

OK, but in fairness, the NTSB stated it couldn't tell which pilot was flying:

Tetrahydrocannabinol carboxylic acid was detected in the blood (0.0071 ug/ml), in the urine (0.071 ug/ml) and in the lung (0.006 ug/ml). Tetrahydrocannabinol carboxylic acid is the inactive metabolite of tetrahydrocannabinol. Additionally, terazosin was detected in the blood and urine. Terazosin is an alpha blocker used to treat benign prostate disease.

We can call this a medical accident. Wonder what the Medicare or VA reports would have said. We do know that getting them would have been no problem at all, just a fax or two.

We also know that once again this was a case in which a pilot with a known severe medical condition was untethered by the FAA from his special issuance and allowed to drop off the radar into the light-sport class, where he eventually died flying an aircraft, even though the FAA had told him seven years prior he wasn't eligible to fly except under special conditions wherein they would require yearly monitoring of his condition.

The medical report completed by the NTSB medical officer mentions no attempt at all at obtaining US government records from Medicare. It does note it did obtain US medical records from the FAA.

For the purposes of advancing medical knowledge and for the purposes of increasing aviation safety, I propose that we stop allowing special issuances to lapse unless the medical condition that we stated was debilitating actually rehabilitates itself. Oh, and don't smoke pot and fly airplanes.

ERA12FA491

In this accident, the seventy-nine-year-old pilot/owner on antidepressants and beta-blockers died when he and his flight instructor crashed in an overloaded aircraft. The pilot had just began flying again after a thirty-year hiatus. No serious attempt at obtaining medical records appears to have happened. Little discussion was wasted on the fine points of a pilot at age seventy-nine suddenly deciding to begin flying again while on antidepressants and a medication for either hypertension or heart disease.

The pilot's obituary mentions that he was discharged honorably from the army, which raises the question regarding VA records being obtainable. Certainly, at age seventy-nine, he likely had Medicare.

CEN12FA638

In this accident, the pilot lost control of the aircraft while maneuvering to land. He was on two sedating antihistamines and was taking antidepressants; however, the NTSB wasn't able to determine if depression significant enough to require medication combined with two sedating medications actually contributed.

I can.

No one in his right mind would fly on two sedating antihistamines and an antidepressant. This accident was medically caused. Sedation and depression cause people to have a reduced skill set and reduced concentration. The evidence of these two parameters is that the pilot lost control of the aircraft while maneuvering to land.

There is no evidence the NTSB made any attempt to ascertain the severity of this elderly gentleman's depression or his other medical issues.

CEN12LA636

A fifty-two-year-old pilot died when he stalled and spun his aircraft on takeoff. While he was taking a decongestant, this medication isn't sedating. No medical history was obtained, and no cause for the accident was found. People usually don't take decongestants if they feel great that day. People usually take decongestants because they aren't 100 percent that day. Did this contribute at all? Was he tired because he was congested all night? Investigating an accident requires these questions to be at least considered.

ERA13LA093

Well, let's just look at the pertinent points for this one.

According to the NTSB medical factual report review of the autopsy results, "the examination of the heart identified atherosclerotic coronary artery disease. The heart weighed 420 grams (normal range for a male of this weight is 281–489 grams). The left ventricular wall measured 1.2 cm (normal). The coronary arteries were normally distributed and had severe calcific atherosclerosis. The amount of vessel occlusion was not recorded. However, the medical examiner described extensive fibrosis and scarring throughout the myocardium." Microscopic evaluation of the heart was not conducted.

Toxicological testing was subsequently performed by the FAA Forensic Toxicology Research Team, Oklahoma City, Oklahoma, which identified amlodipine in liver and blood and valsartan in liver and blood.

The NTSB medical factual report also noted that amlodipine is a blood-pressure medication marketed under the brand name Norvasc and that valsartan is a blood-pressure medication marketed under the brand name Diovan. In addition, the pilot's wife reported that he was using amlodipine and valsartan daily to treat high blood pressure and that he had recently complained of episodes of dizziness.

Now, that is a good start. Actually, that was also where they stopped. Cause of accident per the NTSB was reported as the pilot's impairment or incapacitation due to the effects of medication, worsening cardiac disease, or cardiac arrhythmia, which resulted in his loss of control of the airplane.

The NTSB did assert that this was most likely a medical accident. For thoroughness and also for the protection of the NTSB against claims of libel (or slander), the pilot's past medical records should be gathered.

The past medical records will show how much the pilot knew about his condition, as well as elucidate what the autopsy couldn't. For instance, if the pilot had recently undergone cardiac testing, more information would have been obtained regarding the extent of his cardiac disease as well as his knowledge regarding his health.

ERA13FA219

In this accident a pilot with uncontrolled diabetes and with diphenhydramine, a sedating antihistamine, in his system wrecked and was killed when he attempted his first solo gyrocopter flight in gusty conditions. This pilot's judgment was pathologically impaired.

The NTSB investigator incorrectly stated that the diphenhydramine would likely not have been impairing. This is purely speculative and not based in science, since levels below those the pilot was tested for have been associated with drowsiness. Drowsy isn't the best way to fly, particularly when your blood sugar is out of control, which also means your hydration status will be out of control. It is unclear where the NTSB investigator obtained his medical insights into the impairing nature of diabetes and of diphenhydramine. Wherever he obtained it, it served a purpose: it closed the investigation.

The truth also is that diphenhydramine is often taken for sleep disorders. In other words, by people who are tired and not sleeping well. One of the early signs of diabetes is fatigue.

Yet read the NTSB's probable cause:

> Toxicological testing revealed therapeutic levels of diphenhydramine (for example, Benadryl) in the pilot's blood samples. Diphenhydramine is a sedating antihistamine that could impair a pilot's cognitive and psychomotor performance. The diphenhydramine in cavity blood (0.038 ug/ml) was slightly above the lower limit of the normal therapeutic range (0.0250 to 0.1120 ug/ml). Diphenhydramine undergoes significant postmortem redistribution; as a result, it is likely that the pilot's diphenhydramine level was most likely at or below the lower therapeutic level about the time of the accident. Therefore, it is unlikely that impairment from diphenhydramine degraded the pilot's ability to safely operate the gyroplane.

That is just nonsense.

In the first place, the pilot didn't have the ability to safely operate the gyroplane. He had a chance to prove that he did, and he failed the final exam.

Second, this is a hell of a speculation for an accident investigator to make. Especially someone who is not a health professional. Yet if you examine the docket, there are no other papers that indicate the investigator spoke about this speculation with a physician.

In fact, there are several issues with the diphenhydramine.

1. It is highly sedating, and, in fact, the narrative report for this very accident even says as much:

    > According to the National Highway Traffic Safety Administration report, Drugs and Human Performance Fact Sheets: Diphenhydramine: Diphenhydramine clearly impairs driving performance, and may have an even greater impact than does alcohol on the complex task of operating a motor vehicle. Laboratory studies have shown diphenhydramine to decrease alertness, decrease reaction time, induce somnolence, impair concentration, impair time estimation, impair tracking, decrease learning ability, and impair attention and memory within the first 2–3 hours post dose. Significant adverse effects on vigilance, divided attention, working memory, and psychomotor performance have been demonstrated.

2. There is a *reason* the pilot was taking the medication, which is equally important. Was it for a sleeping issue? Was it for allergies? If you don't even care enough to know why he was taking the medication, why do you care about its side effects? If he was taking it for extreme insomnia, perhaps that tidbit is every bit as big a problem as the medication itself. Before you claim the medication wasn't the problem, you sort of have the obligation to make sure the *reason* for taking the medication wasn't every bit as debilitating to this individual. Otherwise, you just look out of your element.

3. When did he decide to fly? I am no genius, but even I know it would have been before the flight occurred (I'm smart that

way). Thus, at the time he was making decisions, his diphenhydr-amine level would be much higher than after he crashed. Which means that prior to departing his house, he made a decision to fly. And he made the decision while under the impact of a highly sedating medication at higher levels than when he crashed.

4. Diphenhydramine can cause drowsiness at thirty nanograms per milliliter. The pilot's level after the flight and after he died and after the sampling occurred was still more than thirty-eight nanograms per milliliter. It is almost impossible that the diphen-hydramine wasn't impacting him in a negative sense earlier that day when he was making the decision to go to the airport. So the fact that it might not have impaired him during the flight doesn't address that it almost certainly would have been impair-ing him *earlier* when planning the flight.

5. His decision making is that of an impaired thinker. He took off for his first flight in gusty conditions with an aircraft he knew was having a possible mechanical issue. Does this sound like the decision-making process of a person who *isn't* impaired?

The investigator continued:

The clinical findings of an elevated hemoglobin A1C (9.2 percent) and elevated glucose in the urine is consistent with poorly controlled diabetes. The hemoglobin A1C of 9.2 per-cent correlates with an average blood sugar level of about 250 mg/ml (below 140 mg/ml is normal). Blood sugar elevated into this range causes few identified symptoms other than in-creased urination and is not acutely impairing. However, long-term diabetes can cause loss of vision, neuropathy in the lower limbs, and kidney disease. The investigation could not deter-mine if the pilot had any symptoms from diabetes or its long-term complications. Examination of the airframe, engine, and flight control system components revealed no evidence of preimpact mechanical malfunctions or anomalies that would have precluded normal operation.

That simply is nonsense. The investigator made no apparent attempt to see whether the pilot had any medical records. Pilots with a 9.2 hemoglobin A1C blood level will quite often have symptoms of fatigue, depression, thirst, feeling dehydrated, mild confusion, and so on. Stating that increased urination is one of the few identified symptoms ignores the few symptoms that are identifiable—fatigue, depression, and mild confusion, just to name three of the few identified symptoms that every premed student likely knows Does this sound like it might apply here? Just based on the facts, it is almost impossible to believe the pilot wasn't impaired.

The investigator appears to be going out of his way to dispel any impact from a sedating antihistamine and uncontrolled diabetes and made little attempt to contact any treating doctors. It smelled funny to me. The docket had no input from the NTSB medical staff or any documents from an FAA doctor.

I am not big on paranoid theories, but out of literally hundreds of reports I have read, this is the only report I remember where the investigator went out of the way to claim that a disease has few symptoms, while ignoring one of the symptoms that is well known is *fatigue*. Fatigue isn't a good symptom when deciding whether to fly. Additionally, the pilot was taking a medication that is used for people who are *fatigued* and who attribute this fatigue to insomnia. It is also the only NTSB report where an investigator went out of his way to explain why a therapeutic level of diphenhydramine after death would have been probably *nonimpairing* in a pilot. In the vast majority of cases, the investigator will say, "Couldn't be determined."

I may be overthinking this whole issue. The bottom line is that the pilot made a very poor decision that seems predicated by "get-there-itis," and it cost him his life. Based on him having an untreated medical condition that causes fatigue and his use of a medication commonly used for insomnia to help him sleep better and thus feel less fatigued, my finding is that his medical condition almost certainly contributed to his decision making.

But I will leave you and this accident with a cited study and its excerpted objective:

> Fatigue is a common and distressing complaint among people with diabetes, and likely to hinder the ability to perform daily diabetes self-management tasks. A review of the literature about diabetes-related fatigue was conducted with an eye toward creating a framework for beginning to conduct more focused studies on this subject.[3]

It is tragic when the NTSB doesn't gather medical information, but it is ridiculous when it attempts to claim that a 9.2 hemoglobin A1C, which indicates extremely poor diabetic control, is not associated with much significant symptomology. I am thinking NIH might disagree.

I would also add that another meta-analysis found that cognitive decline is found in at least 40 percent of diabetics, and depression was found to be twice as likely in a diabetic population.[4]

Anxiety also is increased in diabetics, with up to 32 percent of diabetics reporting increased anxiety.[5]

The final point on this is: if you are just going to assert that a completely out-of-control diabetic has few symptoms, at least try to read up on the topic and get the pilot's health history. Otherwise, you are going to get called out on it. Because your assertion is simply wrong.

---

3 Cynthia Fritschi and Laurie Quinn, "Fatigue in Patients with Diabetes: A Review," *Journal of Psychosomatic Research* 69, no. 1 (July 2010): 33–41.

4 Nancy Ho, Marilyn S. Sommers, and Irwin Luckib, "Effects of Diabetes on Hippocampal Neurogenesis: Links to Cognition and Depression," *Neurosci Biobehav Rev.* 37, no. 8 (2013): 1346–1362.

5 M. M. Collins, P. Corcoran, and I. J. Perry, "Anxiety and Depression Symptoms in Patients with Diabetes," *Diabet Med.* 26, no. 2 (2009): 153–61. doi: 10.1111/j.1464-5491.2008.02648.x.

11

THE SEDATED, DRUGGED, AND DEPRESSED

DFW07LA102

IN THIS MEDICAL fatality, a pilot took a light-sport airplane off into deteriorating IMC conditions, while on antidepressants and a sedating antihistamine. The sixty-three-year-old man didn't survive. No attempt was made to determine why he was on antidepressants. The lack of judgment by this quite probably depressed, sedated pilot makes this a medically caused fatal airplane accident.

CHI07LA157

This accident is suspicious, as the pilot was on antidepressants and was witnessed pulling up off the runway to a ninety-degree angle before stalling, crashing, and dying. Barring a mechanical issue that the NTSB didn't discover, there are elements to this that suggest suicide. The NTSB didn't look deeply into this pilot's mental issues to find what would have caused him to be on antidepressants. Additionally, a therapeutic dosage of Citalopram would be about fifty to one hundred nanograms per milliliter. This pilot's blood levels were 164 nanograms per milliliter. This could indicate a very recent ingestion or a pilot who inadvertently took his medication at higher than recommended levels. Conjecture is just guessing spelled differently; what would be really helpful would be the decedent's medical records. I would call this a medically caused crash.

CEN10FA182

In this accident, an eighty-year-old man purchased a light-sport amphib. He lost control of his new toy while on diphenhydramine at levels twice the amount at which drowsiness is seen to occur. The impact of sedating medications on the elderly cannot be overstated. After all, hip fractures have been associated with these medications for years. It is most probable the gentleman was suffering from some degree of mental impairment if one believes the National Highway Transportation and Safety Administration reports that mental impairment can occur above sixty nanograms per milliliter. After all, his blood levels were eighty nanograms per milliliter. This is a medically related crash until proven otherwise.

DEN07FA158

In this accident, an instructor took up an overloaded airplane with a student who was taking narcotics, sedating antihistamines, and a blood pressure medication. It is interesting to note that while a medical isn't required for light-sport aircraft, the presence of wakefulness and absence of a condition known to be incompatible to flight is required. No attempt to figure out why the student was on a narcotic or if the student had heart disease was attempted. Despite this, failing to properly preflight an airplane when you and the passenger combined are at the max weight of the useful load makes this a medically caused crash. Judgment is medical.

CEN10FA107

In this accident, an instructor pilot had diphenhydramine in his system at almost six times the dosage necessary to see mental faculty impairment. There is no clear explanation of why the gentleman had diphenhydramine.

Was he excessively obese and couldn't sleep? Did he had severe allergies? What was the reason that he lost control and killed himself and a fifteen-year-old? Did he fall asleep, or was he simply not concentrating because of the highly sedating nature of the medication he was taking?

Let's see the two things the NTSB could come up with:

The FAA's Civil Aerospace Medical Institute, Oklahoma City, Oklahoma, performed toxicological tests on specimens that were collected during the autopsy. Results were negative for carbon monoxide, cyanide, and ethanol. Testing of the blood revealed 0.159 ug/ml diphenhydramine. Diphenhydramine is a sedating antihistamine which is commonly used in the treatment of allergies and the common cold.

The National Transportation Safety Board determines the probable cause(s) of this accident as follows: A loss of aircraft control while maneuvering for undetermined reasons.

Interesting.

So the gentleman was on a sleeping aid/anti-allergy medication used ubiquitously around the world to put people to sleep.

"Effective antihistamine concentrations are greater than 25 ng/mL, drowsiness can be observed at 30–40 ng/mL, and mental impairment may be observed with concentrations above 60 ng/mL" (www.nhtsa.gov/people/injury/research/job185drugs/diphenhydramine.htm).

According to the National Highway Transportation and Safety Administration, the pilot would possibly have been drowsy at thirty to forty nanograms per milliliter and mentally impaired above sixty. The pilot was flying at a blood level of 159 nanograms per milliliter.

Probable cause? I'd say he was, according to the US government, probably mentally impaired—a lot. That would be the same US government that couldn't find the cause of the accident, by the way.

I'd like to say this was all fantasy and that stuff like this could never possibly happen, but this group, alleging to be accident-investigation experts, who charge three thousand dollars or more to train people in one week so they too can be experts, was handed a toxicology report showing a pilot had five times the level of diphenhydramine in his system necessary to cause sedation, and nobody commented on the probability that he was markedly impaired.

A fifteen-year-old died. There has to be some amount of culpability, but we all assume these experts are doing their jobs, when it has become remarkably obvious that they are not.

This is the time to refute some obvious rebuttals that are sure to be thrown my way:

"It would be cost prohibitive, Dr. Shewmaker."

Uh, you were handed results showing that you had a pilot with five times the limit of diphenhydramine in his system sufficient to cause drowsiness. You have a medical staff, and presumably you get free access to the PDR in the Library of Congress. *Do your job*, and by the way, please learn the meaning of *probable*.

"Diphenhydramine is redistributed in patients upon their death."

Fair enough, but why was he taking a sedating antihistamine? Explain what symptoms this gentleman had that would cause him to want to take sedating antihistamines. Oh, you didn't bother to find out the symptoms or the issues the pilot had? Explain how long ago he took the medication, and whether that was during his flight-planning period, meaning he would have been mentally impaired while planning his go/no-go decision process.

Rebuttals rebutted. The issue isn't cost, and it isn't redistribution. The issue is the NTSB isn't investigating these accidents with any modicum of a protocol, a plan, or a commitment to the facts.

CEN10LA526

In this fatal accident, a pilot with a fairly high level of diphenhydramine in his system and with two hours of flight time in the past ninety days decided to go flying in his newly built airplane for the very first time. It was also the last time.

The total flight experience of the pilot was seventy-six hours, including eight total hours in a similar airframe. The concept of being a test pilot without any real significant experience while being on a high dose of a sedative makes this pretty clearly a medically related crash.

The forty-eight-year-old pilot's blood level of diphenhydramine was 164 nanograms per milliliter. The pilot was also taking naproxen and ibuprofen. A level of sixty nanograms per milliliter of diphenhydramine has been found to be sufficient to cause mental impairment. His levels were just a bit more than that.

As you can see, a lot of fatal accidents occurred with pilots on sedating medications they can buy over the counter. There may be a need for a focused education effort on the dangers of these medications, especially if you are going to let people with known severe medical conditions fly passengers who are being hoodwinked into thinking these pilots are healthy.

12

THE SAND IS WARM—WHY
BOTHER TO INVESTIGATE?

THIS CHAPTER REFLECTS accidents wherein the investigations have all wrapped up. The animals are back in the barn. Yet, if we reflect on what was investigated and what was not, we quickly realize that full investigations simply weren't fully attempted.

CEN09LA312

In this accident, two persons died owing to a loss of control; the NTSB didn't find a cause.

ERA09LA369

In this accident, two more people died as a result of a loss of control; the NTSB didn't find a cause.

LAX07LA175

In this accident, the pilot was testing his experimental aircraft and lost control of the plane, resulting in his death. No attempt to obtain medical or psychological medical history was apparently attempted. This crash is unclear.

MIA07LA136

In this flight, the NTSB found that the pilot exceeded the abilities of the aircraft, subsequently resulting in a breakup in flight. Two persons were killed. No attempt to assess whether the pilot had some mental issue that would have caused him to possess poor judgment appears to have been attempted. The human factors behind this accident thus are not clear.

LAX08LA050

In this accident, in which two people were killed, a flight instructor was apparently giving a new student his first introduction to light-sport aircraft. It is unclear whether the instructor knew that he had a damaged heart and severe heart disease, since the NTSB made no clear attempt to obtain his past medical records.

The autopsy report noted:

Toxicology tests were performed on specimens from both pilots. No evidence of drugs or ethanol was found. The autopsies revealed both pilots were killed due to multiple blunt force traumatic injuries. The coroner noted that the flight instructor had evidence of ischemic heart disease, with severe coronary atherosclerosis and myocardial fibrosis.

Does the student's family have a right to know what the instructor knew about his own health? Was the instructor one of those types who simply never went to the physician? There are a lot of unanswered questions. Worse, the autopsy gave the NTSB a starting point, even if up to that point, it wasn't going to bother attempting to get records. Now the autopsy report is hanging in its face and it still evidently couldn't be bothered.

No need for a medical; go take an introductory flight.

MIA08LA090

In this accident, it is completely unclear whether there was a medical issue or not. The student pilot had no logbook, and no apparent attempt was made to find out who was instructing the sixty-three-year-old, since there were no endorsements found that would have made this a legal student-pilot flight. The lack of a medical records search is par for the course.

MIA08LA105

In this accident, there was no clear reason for the airplane crash. The NTSB found that it crashed due to some unknown reason. Toxicology was negative; a search for any information about the pilot's medical or mental history doesn't appear to have been accomplished.

LAX08LA181

In this accident, a fifty-nine-year-old was killed when he crashed during his first solo flight. He was transported to a hospital but succumbed. No serious effort to obtain his medical records was recorded.

WPR10FA223

In this accident, the pilot and the wreck were not found for seven months after his airplane disappeared. Obviously, toxicology wasn't of value. No attempt to identify past medical issues was made.

CEN10LA031

In this accident, in which the pilot and the passenger both died, the airplane appeared to stall while turning slowly. The NTSB reported that eight months prior to the accident, the pilot had had two coronary stents placed, but since then he had resumed all activity (per his family). At no time does it appear the investigators attempted to ascertain the extent of the coronary-artery disease, the severity of it, the prognosis, or any cardiology records that might have shed light on whether this was the only medical issues that pilot had, or whether he had had further incidents of angina after the stent placement. It may be a "bent mirror," but it is part of doing a full investigation.

WPR09FA005

This one is suspicious because of sudden incapacitation, but despite having the opportunity to dig, the NTSB stopped at the beginning instead of at the end of a thorough investigation. The seventy-year-old flight instructor and his student were flying at one thousand feet. According to the student:

> In a written statement, the PUI reported that he and the instructor had flown up the coast with no problems noted. The PUI recalled returning to Santa Monica at about 1,000 feet offshore and straight and level. The next thing that he recalled was being in the water.

So they were flying along perfectly; then they were in the water. What does this sound like? It sounds like a sudden event.

> The injuries of the CFI were documented in the medical records and obtained by the NTSB from the University of California, Los Angeles Medical Center. The pilot succumbed to his injuries seventeen days following the accident. According to the University of California, Los Angeles Medical Center, the pilot sustained carotid artery dissection, a bilateral subdural hematoma, a frontal subarachnoid hemorrhage and edema, fractures of the T11, L4, left first rib fracture, lateral left third to fifth rib fractures, with a substernal hematoma to the right anterior, third rib fracture, and injuries to the head and chest.

That is it.

The NTSB had the chance. It obtained the UCLA Medical Center records. Those records would have certainly listed the injuries, but the injuries aren't part of the accident cause investigation. The injuries happened *after* the cause of the loss of control, not before it. The NTSB didn't look at causes; it looked only at the *results* of the crash. The rib fractures, carotid dissection, subarachnoid hemorrhage, and so on didn't *cause* the accident. An accident investigation that looks only at the injuries and not the causes is fascinatingly morbid but serves absolutely no purpose. The NTSB might have just as well described his tattoos in detail, for all the benefit to the cause of this accident.

Now, what also would have been in those seventeen days of hospital medical records?

- His insurance information, probably Medicare and/or VA
- His medical history
- His medication lists
- His surgical history
- The name of his primary-care physician
- The names of his specialist physicians

Why were the injuries that were caused by the accident investigated and the potential causes of the accident not investigated? One can only presume that the NTSB either has no idea what to look for during an accident investigation or that it has no protocol for properly training accident investigators. It is as if they have no checklist.

CEN10FA042

This accident demonstrates why one should be very cautious in one's word choice on an accident investigation, but I think it is best to avoid being too judgmental as well. Mistakes happen.

The seventy-one-year-old pilot had a medical condition that the FAA three years prior had told him was incompatible with flying. However, under the special issuance process, the FAA allowed the pilot to fly, as long as he had regular monitoring. At no time did the NTSB comment on what this grounding medical condition was. One can make a reasonable guess, however, based on the fact that the pilot was on a beta-blocker medication as well as an ARB-class antihypertensive. The most likely choice of a geriatric pilot on two antihypertensive medications, one of which is rate controlling, is a heart condition. Other possible choices of why the pilot at age seventy-one was on a special issuance, might have been prostate cancer that had been treated. We'll never know.

The light-sport rule allowed this pilot to stop having the FAA require him to have regular follow-up with his treating physician. The light-sport rule allowed this pilot to simply continue flying, and there was zero requirement for him, with his known grounding medical condition, to ever have any further treatment for that condition. The NTSB makes a glaring error in its narrative report:

> Medical and pathological examination of the pilot revealed the cause of death as impact related and no medical or toxicological issues that would have precluded him from operating the airplane in a safe manner prior to the accident.

This isn't a true assessment. There was no medical examination listed in the NTSB docket. There was only an autopsy report and a toxicology report. Beta-blockers certainly could have caused a pilot to have issues with controlling an airplane, as could the reason for which the beta-blocker was prescribed. The very presence of a special issuance having been placed on the pilot on his last FAA medical demonstrates that there was at least one medical issue that would have precluded him from operating the airplane in a safe manner—in fact, the first paragraph of every special issuance states as much.

A much more accurate statement would have been: "This was an in-flight breakup event. We didn't attempt to determine who this pilot's primary physician or cardiologist was, even though both of these persons would have almost certainly been listed in the FAA medical examination done only two and a half years earlier. We additionally made no attempt to contact these medical professionals, obtain any medical records whatsoever, and have no idea if the pilot was taking beta-blockers for the first time and had an adverse reaction to them that very day. We additionally do not know if he wasn't taking medication that he had been prescribed, such as a narcotic, because we didn't bother to look for such information in any way, shape, or form."

This may seem overly harsh, but let's read the NTSB comments on the pilot:

> The pilot, age 71, held a sport pilot certificate issued on January 12, 2008. In addition, he held a repairman certificate for light sport aircraft—Zodiac 601 XL, N538CJ. He was issued a third-class airman medical certificate/student pilot certificate on July 24, 2007. The medical certificate contained the limitations "holder must wear corrective lenses" and "not valid for any class after May 31, 2008." The pilot held a valid driver's license for the state of Illinois.

The only time there is a statement such as "not valid for any class..." on an FAA medical is when there is a medical condition so severe that the FAA determines that pilot is not qualified to fly but will be allowed to do so under the special condition that the FAA regularly monitors the health condition by making the pilot regularly send it medical records. These medical records would have contained the names of the pilot's treating physicians. An investigation that wasn't simply looking for a reason to close a book on a wreck would have looked directly at this "not valid for any class..." and asked the following five questions:

1. Who were the pilot's doctors?
2. What was he being treated for?
3. How good a patient was he?
4. How bad was his condition?
5. Had it decompensated?

In fairness, this likely was a mechanically related accident. The mechanic for this airplane was the pilot. Remember him? We were just discussing him a moment ago. Something about him having a known medical condition so severe that the FAA had previously put him on a special issuance. His health was a part of the investigation, regardless of whether the wreck was the result of mechanical issues (he was the mechanic) or pilot error (he was the pilot).

This once again points to the fact that the NTSB will focus on aircraft design and function to a degree that is admirable, while simultaneously missing out on the point that the oldest piece of equipment on the aircraft was the pilot/mechanic, and the pilot/mechanic had a known mechanical defect that the US government (FAA) had documented and quite probably Medicare and/or the VA had also documented.

Additionally, despite the focus on the mechanics rather than the human factors, the NTSB seems not to consider the human factors of the mechanics. This pilot was the mechanic. Thus, his physical and mental fitness as a mechanic is equally as important as his physical and mental fitness as a pilot.

Witness this comment:

Structures Study
For this study, NTSB investigators conducted extensive examination of the airplane wreckage from this accident and other similar accidents. In addition, NTSB investigators referred to the results of flight and static testing, accident investigation reports,

and special studies conducted by several investigative and certification authorities from the United States, United Kingdom, Netherlands, and Germany.

Again let's note that the pilot was the oldest structure on the aircraft, and you didn't need to read European studies; you simply had to ask for the medical information from the same person you checked with regarding the pilot's medical certificate (the FAA) and use that information to obtain the pilot's medical doctor's contact information.

None of this negates the fact that this particular accident was possibly caused by a design flaw.

Following are some further NTSB quotes:

Ultimately both wings failed in down bending at the root. The ailerons did not have counterbalances that offer direct protection from aerodynamic flutter. Aerodynamic flutter can occur when there is insufficient stiffness in the structure or the flight controls are not mass balanced.

The accident pilot was experienced in the accident airplane and had built the airplane from a kit.

After several accidents in Europe, the United Kingdom Light Aircraft Association designed and flight tested ailerons fitted with counter balances. Counter balances are considered a more direct mitigation strategy to prevent aileron flutter.

A review of the Experimental Aircraft Association (EAA) safety program records revealed that the owner/builder had not participated in either the EAA Flight Adviser or the EAA Technical Counselor Programs.

Did the mechanic appear to be up on the most current information regarding airframe safety on the aircraft on which he worked? Did he relay this up-to-date information to the pilot (himself)?

At the very least, one investigating an accident regarding an elderly gentleman who designed and built an airplane might consider that the airplane mechanic's competency and mental status would be areas to explore. Certainly, unless one bothered to look, it would be somewhat reckless to declare, "Medical and pathological examination of the pilot revealed the cause of death as impact related and no medical or toxicological issues that would have precluded him from operating the airplane in a safe manner prior to the accident."

This is totally inaccurate. There wasn't any real medical examination other than an autopsy. No mental exam, no physical exam, no search of his actual insurance records, no search of his medications that he should have been taking but possibly refused to take, and so on. Medical examination occurs on live people, autopsies on the dead. Perhaps this was just poor word choice.

As for the precise question of how good a mechanic the pilot was:

The airplane registered to and operated by the pilot was maintained under an annual condition inspection program. The maintenance records were not with the airplane wreckage. Several requests were sent to the owner's estate, requesting that the maintenance records and airplane information, or copies of those records and information be provided to the National Transportation Safety Board (NTSB) for their review. These records were not located by the bank handling the estate. Requests sent to family members were not responded to.

Seems like the family didn't want to be bothered with such details. And this speaks volumes about the possibility of a medical issue underlying this pilot's accident. When insurance, lawyers, and estates become involved, families who are smart enough to realize a pilot has a reason he or she shouldn't fly will clam up. But insurance records, medical records, and hospital records won't clam up. And therein is where the NTSB is sleeping on its pillow.

One point is crystal clear: the NTSB investigator didn't mention what medical condition the pilot had three years prior that required the FAA to tell the pilot that the FAA had determined he was "ineligible for medical certification under Title 14, Code of Federal Regulations (CFRS)."

CEN10FA278

This was an accident on landing. Haven't seen one of those for a bit. In this case the seventy-six-year-old pilot, with over 1,600 flight hours, told witnesses before he expired that the cockpit canopy had opened during the landing sequence, causing a loss of control. Little else can be gleaned that would provide further commentary, as the only items on the NTSB docket related to medical issues were the toxicology screening and a mention of the fact that he'd had a medical in 2006.

Left off the report was that he was under a special restriction on the 2006 medical examination and also left off was the medical condition that placed him under this special restriction. While page five of the NTSB factual report alludes to these issues, it doesn't spell out what these issues were. Perhaps a cognitive decline? Without information, we are simply forced to guess.

ERA10FA435

The next accident was another such case. A highly experienced pilot, age seventy-seven, new toy, taking passenger for a ride, wrecks, killing both. Negative toxicology screen, no medical records. The family searched for answers, but, in a twist, at least one family member stated that they believed he may have become incapacitated. Although the son reported more than a year after the accident that he was still baffled because his father evidently was in excellent health. The truth may be that he never had any preventative screening, and thus an avoidable issue was missed. The other truth may be that this simply was an elderly gentleman becoming incapacitated while doing what he loved. *May* is simply another word for *guess*. A lack of a good accident investigation will leave a lot of room for such guessing.

WPR10FA435

Here the instructor pilot overbanked the aircraft while at a low altitude, killing himself and injuring the student. The pilot had cold medication in his system and was age forty-five. There is little discussion of his weight, BMI, and so on. The report states the autopsy wasn't useful in identifying any medical issues.

CEN11LA012

In this accident, a "student" pilot killed a passenger—I think. The NTSB narrative calls the pilot the student. The probable-cause report calls the passenger a student. There is no logbook for either. The entire two paragraphs of the narrative were practically cut and pasted into the probable-cause report. I could just as well throw a dart and imagine what caused the accident with equally efficacious results.

To demonstrate my point, I will copy the entire NTSB narrative report here:

*** Note: NTSB investigators may not have traveled in support of this investigation and used data provided by various sources to prepare this aircraft accident report. ***

On October, 8, 2010, about 1330 central daylight time, a Challenger II, light-sport airplane, N61328, impacted terrain following a loss of control near Easton, Kansas. The student rated pilot was fatally injured, the sole passenger received serious injuries, and the aircraft was substantially damaged. The airplane was registered to and operated by a private individual. Visual meteorological conditions prevailed and the personal flight was being conducted under the provisions of 14 Code of Federal Regulations (CFR) Part 91. The flight originated from a private airfield around 1300. There were no reported witnesses to the accident. A passer-by noticed the wreckage near a rural road, heard the passenger's call for help, and notified authorities. In an interview conducted by a Federal Aviation Administration (FAA) inspector, the passenger stated that they departed the pilot's property around 1300–1330, and was only airborne for about 10 minutes. The passenger added that the pilot expressed a concern about the wind and decided they needed to return to the airfield. During the turn back to the airfield, the passenger felt like they were losing altitude and may have encountered a downdraft. The pilot suddenly told him to "hang on" and activated the airplane's parachute. The passenger further stated that he was sure the engine was running, but he could not recall the impact sequence and he estimated the airplane was about 350 feet above ground level, when they started the turn. The responding FAA inspector reported that the airplane impacted the tops of several trees before coming to rest at the base of the trees. The aircraft was equipped with a ballistic parachute system, and the parachute was entangled with the tops of the trees. The inspector also reported that the fuel tank was about half-full of fuel. The inspector added that a part of the tail section was located about 75 feet from the main wreckage.

Examination of the wreckage revealed that the parachute had deployed; however, it appeared that the chute was not fully opened prior to the airplane impact with the ground. The airplane's control cables/rods appeared intact and connected. The engine would rotate by hand, and appeared normal. A visual inspection of the drive belts, throttle cable, and carburetors did not reveal any discrepancies. The right section of the stabilizer/elevator, located away from the wreckage did not have any impact marks on its tube framing, and the fabric appeared in good shape. Two bolts holding the section on were broken, and were removed for further examination.

Both bolts were sent to the Safety Board Materials Laboratory in Washington, DC, for examination. The Materials Laboratory factual report noted that both bolts had "bending and a cupped fracture face, consistent with a bending overload event." The pilot's flight log and airplane maintenance records were not located in the course of this investigation.

Wow.

The NTSB spends the majority of the investigation looking at whether the bolts that were obviously overloaded during the loss of control exhibited any signs of being overloaded. The investigators didn't bother at all with the pilot, his toxicology, his medical records, anything. It gets worse. (I get the feeling I am saying that entirely too much.)

This accident has no reports listed on the NTSB docket, no report of an autopsy, no report of toxicology, and it is the end result of an investigation that apparently took nine months to complete. Personally, I think I could have made this accident report up over a morning coffee with just about as much effort.

I can tell you one other thing that isn't in the NTSB reports. The pilot died in hospice six months after the accident. Getting medical records would have been fairly easy if the NTSB had bothered. The name of the hospice was listed in his obituary, and his death occurred two months before the NTSB finished its investigation.

It is nice to know that the NTSB investigated what occurred with the bolts of the aircraft *after* the pilot lost control. I can say fairly confidently that if it wants to go back and investigate the paint job, that it has a high likelihood of being more faded as well.

When you can find out more about a pilot on Google than in an NTSB report, you realize the NTSB isn't as interested in investigating accidents as you might be.

WPR11LA069

In this accident, a seventy-year-old man was killed. He lost control of his aircraft, and it crashed. He had aspirin in his system. That is the extent of the NTSB investigation on a gentleman who was a retired elementary school principal.

Retired school principals will likely have an insurance policy related to their prior employment, or it is likely the pilot was on Medicare. The information is out there; it is a matter of having a bit of curiosity. Some would call it doing your job.

WPR11FA138

In this accident, the instructor pilot was witnessed to have pulled the aircraft up into a steeply pitched angle after the engine seemed to have experienced a loss and then regaining of power. There was a loss of control, and the aircraft crashed into the ocean, killing both occupants. No medical cause was identified.

ERA11LA263

In this accident, the pilot evidently took up a light-sport aircraft on his first flight in that particular airplane. The questions you might have about this fifteen-hundred-plus-hour pilot and his first experience with this aircraft are never answered by the NTSB. It makes a great teaser sentence. But where is the meat? The tox screen was negative. As usual, the autopsy report wasn't placed in the docket, but it was reportedly normal. The decedent worked for the Army Corps of Engineers, so there wasn't a whole lot of reasons the NTSB couldn't have gotten his past medical records if it had so desired. I am thinking that figuring out the insurance carrier for the Army Corps of Engineers isn't likely to be that difficult.

The NTSB's probable cause:

> The pilot's loss of airplane control while taxiing, which resulted in the weight-shift-controlled airplane becoming inadvertently airborne and subsequently impacting the ground. Contributing to the accident was the pilot's lack of experience in the make and model of the accident airplane.

Also: "The pilot's total weight-shift-control airplane flight experience consisted of 5.7 hours flown with a flight instructor in another model airplane."

It would be nice to see if he had had any prior medical or mental-health issues, but without any real evidence of a medical cause, we will simply call this a taxi test gone bad.

ERA11FA413

The next accident occurred when a pilot, towing a glider, crashed immediately after takeoff. The glider crew members were not impacted. No cause was determined by the NTSB, although it conjectured that perhaps the pilot was distracted. Ironically, it could put that into every report as boilerplate, along with perhaps the pilot was thinking about buying a pet. "I don't know" is the right answer when you don't know.

CEN11FA531

In this accident, the NTSB investigator showed zero interest at all in exploring any medical issues. A pilot self-reporting form, four-page interview by a sheriff's detective, and six photos represented the entire amount of significance the NTSB placed on the death of the passenger, who died as a result of pilot error. More thought was likely given to what type of coffee the investigator would order that week. The fact that it wasn't a New York Yankee or a senator who died likely explains why twelve NTSB personnel didn't jet down from Washington to investigate this rural Wisconsin death by pilot error. Yet, if we are going to actually investigate accidents for the purposes of improving safety, pilot error on takeoff happens a lot more often than flying into an East River apartment by orders of magnitude.

ERA12LA537

The pilot overstressed the aircraft, causing a crash in Ocala, Florida. There was no significant finding on the fifty-year-old's toxicology screening, and no medical records were obtained.

CEN12FA601

The honesty of some narrative reports makes this book far more macabrely fascinating.

Per the NTSB:

Accident site photographs, medical records, as well as autopsy, and toxicological reports were reviewed by the National Transportation Safety Board (NTSB) Chief Medical Officer, in an effort to determine the extent and severity of the pilot's injuries.

He was dead. That takes care of the severity part.

There is no real value to determining the extent and severity of a pilot's injuries in a high-velocity collision with the ground. The value of autopsy and toxicology reports is in helping institute recommendations regarding future aviation-safety requirements. Knowing what all we broke when we dropped the egg off the tower doesn't make the egg one bit more airworthy in the next attempt. I am assuming this is just a poorly chosen set of words.

Then again, it is actually what the NTSB appears to be doing rather than working toward actually understanding the true causatives of accidents.

The next words in the narrative were the following: "According to medical records released to the NTSB by the pilot's family."

This brings up the question about whether the NTSB realizes that it doesn't need the family to release the medical records. It has federal law granting it the power to obtain those records. I guarantee those records are at the decedent's doctor's offices and hospitals and not part of the family estate.

The point I am making here is that this narrative implies that the NTSB needed to ask the family for the medical records. There is no such requirement. So does the NTSB think that there is? *Is* that why it rarely bothers to obtain medical records? It doesn't even know its own strength?

The NTSB narrative didn't even go into detail at all about the pilot's medical conditions; instead it simply limited the entire medical discussion to what happened to the pilot's body after it hit the ground at a high rate of speed.

To wit:

Pilot Injuries
Accident site photographs, medical records, as well as autopsy, and toxicological reports were reviewed by the National Transportation Safety Board (NTSB) Chief Medical Officer, in an effort to determine the extent and severity of the pilot's injuries. According to medical records released to the NTSB by the pilot's family, the pilot was found with a decreased level of consciousness, responding only to painful stimulation. On arrival to the hospital, the following injuries were identified: a posterior dislocation of his left hip prosthesis with a fracture of

the hip socket (acetabulum), a fracture of his left elbow (olec-ranon), bruising of the soft tissue around his right eye with a fracture of the floor of the orbit, compartment syndrome in his right forearm, and "bruising over bilateral shoulders, right greater than left with associated right sided bruising over lateral chest, abdomen, hip"; the physician notes remarked "seat-belt sign."

According to Computerized Tomography (CT) scan of his head, he had bleeding around and swelling within his brain.

Thus, we know he had an artificial hip before the plane crashed. That was all the NTSB figured out when investigating this accident for medical causes. They figured out the results quite well.

But that isn't the purpose of an accident investigation. You aren't concerned with the scrapes on the oak tree; you are concerned with why the car left the road.

When we actually dig into the NTSB docket records, however, this is what the NTSB medical officer stated about the pilot's past records, which the family was kind enough to grant them access to even though family kindness isn't a prerequisite for the NTSB to get these records:

> According to the emergency department records, the pilot's wife reported he had longstanding atrial fibrillation for which he had been placed on an anticoagulant. In addition, he had undergone a hip replacement, had hypertension, and had had multiple stents placed into his coronary arteries to treat coronary artery disease. She reported that at the time of the crash he was taking Coumadin (generically known as warfarin, an anticoagulant to prevent clots), Crestor (generically known as rosuvastatin, a cholesterol lowering agent), and Lisinopril (a calcium channel blocker used to treat hypertension, marketed under the trade names Zestril and Prinivil).

A bit different, ain't it?

Let's recap: a seventy-nine-year-old male with severe coronary-artery disease, artificial hip, hypertension, and atrial fibrillation, on a blood thinner, anticholesterol medication, and blood pressure medication wrecked his airplane, killing himself and seriously injuring another person. That is a bit more to the point. Now knock yourself out describing the outcome at your leisure.

As for the accident's probable cause: "The pilot's failure to maintain airspeed following a partial loss of engine power for reasons that could not be determined during postaccident examination, which resulted in an aerodynamic stall and loss of airplane control."

Maybe, just maybe, his atrial fibrillation, severe coronary-artery disease, and advanced age played a role? I'd say it was almost a certainty, but that is just me. We'll leave this one hanging out there in the "nonmedical" category.

ERA13LA020

Two people died in the next accident, which occurred in Florida. The pilot, age sixty, took off in gusty conditions and promptly crashed the airplane. Other than blood pressure medication found by the FAA in the toxicology screen, there is no indication of what the pilot's medical history was.

WPR13LA313

In June 2013, a fifty-nine-year-old pilot wrecked while flying low down a river, pulling up to avoid wires, and losing control. The toxicology screening was negative. The entire NTSB investigation docket consisted of four interviews with witnesses who saw the pilot waving at them while flying at a very low altitude. The NTSB report was three pages long. No attempt was made to determine if this gentleman was bipolar, off his medications, and thus flying as if he were invincible. The evidence is all there to begin down that route. One year after the accident, the NTSB used its three pages of documents to conclude that the pilot was flying too low, turned too sharply, and crashed. Any of the four witnesses could have done that for the general public and in fact did so—within minutes.

The pilot lived in a town with three thousand residents. His medical records were not obtained.

CEN13LA409

In this fatal accident, two pilots crashed when they encountered strong gusting wind during landing. The flight instructor was killed, and the other licensed pilot, who was undergoing instruction, survived. Both pilots were in their seventies and were on blood pressure medications. No other medical information was gathered as part of the investigation. An autopsy was reported on the pilot. No autopsy information was included in the narrative.

ERA14LA329

The seventy-eight-year-old pilot of this example apparently experienced an issue with an autopilot that had been installed in his aircraft, wrecking just after takeoff. Although he spent eleven days in the hospital, giving the NTSB ample opportunity to assess his medical history, the investigators didn't.

WPR14FA381

A sixty-nine-year-old man died when he failed to recover from a spin, according to the NTSB report, based on collected data from the onboard sensors. No attempt was made to see if this pilot was suffering from any mental illness.

He hadn't flown for many years and had just resumed flying, accumulating about twenty hours, most of it with an instructor.

What you can find within five minutes on the Internet: He is reported by friends to have suffered from PTSD and was involved in a near-fatal helicopter accident decades ago. He also was in Vietnam. A sixty-nine-year-old man involved in combat in Vietnam almost certainly would have some VA records if not Medicare ones. As I've mentioned, you have to want to find answers; it's a prerequisite to a real investigation.

CEN15LA004

A sixty-one-year-old man died in this flight when he flew into a wire. He had decongestants, antacids, and ibuprofen in his system, but no medical records were obtained. Two people died, including the pilot. There was no exploration of whether he routinely flew into areas with inherent dangers without fully scouting them.

ANC13FA095

In this accident, a pilot lost control of his aircraft and crashed, killing himself and seriously injuring a passenger. The sixty-six-year-old pilot's medical records were stated as not located. I wonder if Medicare knows they were looking.

WPR14FA234

"The pilot's steep right turn shortly after takeoff, which led to the airplane exceeding its critical angle-of-attack and experiencing an aerodynamic stall." This was the probable-cause report finding. An eighty-two-year-old and a sixty-six-year-old died. The eighty-two-year-old did have two blood pressure medications on his toxicology screening.

We have exhausted the list of accidents that aren't all that clear as to the reason the airplane crashed, and we see that accident investigators aren't really going to that much effort to get to the facts. Chapter 13 is in the wheelhouse of the NTSB. It explores the mechanically related accidents. While you read the chapter, also ask yourself this: When pilots are healthy, do they have a better chance of surviving an emergency?

13

MECHANICAL, BUT WHO BUILT THE AIRPLANE?

WPR09LA453

IN THE NEXT accident, an aircraft lost control and crashed while attempting to land. While the rear-seat passenger had insulin-dependent diabetes, the person in the front seat of the tandem aircraft was believed to be the pilot. The toxicology screen was negative for this pilot, who was sixty-eight years of age and weighed 232 pounds. This really is the extent of what the NTSB reported in its docket of accident information.

Mechanically we get some clues about the pilot's mind-set regarding safety:

> The tailwheel assembly was noted affixed to the aft fuselage with household "drywall" screws. An automotive paper type fuel filter was observed in-line with the fuel tank pickup. The Rotax 503 installation manual expressly prohibits the use of paper fuel filters. Multiple drilled holes were observed throughout the fuselage and wing load-bearing structures; these holes did not correspond to locations referenced in the airplane plans. Varying degrees of corrosion were noted on multiple parts throughout the airplane.

Examples of corroded areas included the vertical stabilizer and its fuselage attach points, main landing gear brake and hub assemblies, and fuselage mounted wing strut support structures. The use of "Duct Tape" was noted as a material for sealing the wing/flaperon gap.

But with no real idea what was going on in the pilot's medical history, simply damning this pilot because he used duct tape and drywall screws to keep his corroded aircraft in flying trim seems a bit harsh. Then again, maybe it doesn't.

What I do know is that when you are a pilot, and you preflight an aircraft, and you then fly that aircraft, you are either sane or you are not. You judge for yourself on whether flying this airplane was the act of a sane individual. What I can tell you is you will have done more accident investigation into the human factors of this accident than the NTSB appears to have documented doing just by reading these sentences.

NYC08FA158

In this accident, a mechanical failure resulted in the airplane wrecking. There was not an attempt made by NTSB to look seriously at any underlying pilot medical issues.

LAX08LA160

In this accident, a seventy-six-year-old died when the airplane he built had the builder (himself) fail to install the vertical fin properly. The NTSB report mentioned that he had a medical issue when it noted he had an exam with the FAA two years previously that had waivers and limitations, but it didn't mention what these waivers and limitations were. No attempt to look into his medical history appears to have been made. This is unfortunate. So which came first, the mechanic or the mechanical failure?

WPR09FA141

In this accident, a thirty-seven-year-old pilot was killed when the airplane wings collapsed. No medical causes associated with the accident were presented.

ERA09FA273

In this accident, a Canadian experimental airplane that apparently wasn't welded together too well decided to demonstrate its lack of airworthiness during a cross-country. The builder/owner died. There were no medical records provided except for a negative toxicology screen. No evaluation of the mental or physical competencies of the pilot/builder appears to have been attempted.

CEN10LA050

In this accident, an eighty-one-year-old pilot was killed when an improper sealant was used to seal a fuel leak, resulting in contamination of the fuel. It isn't clear whether the pilot had any preexisting conditions, and his last FAA medical was four years prior. The use of the sealant was not done by the pilot but by the previous owner, who didn't log that he used the improper sealant. It is most likely that the eighty-one-year-old decedent had no idea of an improper sealant being used. The decedent was a retired military officer, so obtaining medical records would have been quite simple, were there a protocol in place to follow the NTSB's mandate to research such information.

Given that this was a fuel contamination issue, this would be a non-medically caused accident.

CEN11LA049

An improperly seated primer, resulting in too rich of a mixture, is reported as the probable cause of this accident. The sixty-six-year-old pilot was the sole fatality. The NTSB studiously avoided studying any underlying medical issues that may have been lurking.

CEN12FA217

In this accident, a fifty-six-year-old pilot with more than three thousand hours lost control of his aircraft and crashed. Engine issues were suspected and explored as a result of a report prior to the most recent annual inspection.

> Due to the violent nature of the impact, the Belmont County Coroner's office was unable to conduct an autopsy on the pilot.
>
> The FAA Bioaeronautical Sciences Research Laboratory, Oklahoma City, Oklahoma, could not perform toxicological tests on the specimens for carbon monoxide or cyanide. The specimens were negative for ethanol and tested drugs.

Uh…correction: the FAA only had muscle to test; therefore, tests for drugs in blood or urine or the liver wasn't possible. Overstating a total lack of evidence could be misleading.

Probable cause? "The loss of engine power and the pilot's diverted attention to the engine power loss, which resulted in a rapid descent and impact with terrain."

Medical factors? Not explored—at all.

Mechanical issues aren't usually the problem when it comes to fatal general-aviation accidents. The human factors are where your most probable cause will be.

14

The Appetizer Sampler: Drugs, Criminality, Disease, Competency? I'll Have One of Each!

T HIS CHAPTER DEALS with the worst of the worst: combinations of criminality, disease, and drugs.

NYC08LA225

In this accident, a pilot illegally took up a passenger despite having no pilot's certificate and despite overloading the aircraft. He was also on a sedating medication as well as an amphetamine. Despite the fact he was on two prescription medications, no search of pharmacy, medical, or insurance records appears to have been attempted.

In the nonsensical *Alice in Wonderland* world of make-believe accident investigations, the NTSB probable-cause report earns a gold star and a Mad Hatter's cup of red zinger:

> The airplane was at least 72 pounds over the 1,100 pound maximum gross weight at the time of the accident. Additionally, the pilot had substantial risk factors for obstructive sleep apnea (marked obesity and evidence of poorly controlled high blood

pressure), had recently taken a prescription sleep aid, and was taking a prescription weight loss product. Given these factors, the pilot's decision making may have been impaired by fatigue, or by the effects of the medications. However, the investigation was unable to verify whether the pilot was impaired during the accident.

What other evidence do you need? He was a noncertificated pilot illegally taking a passenger on a flight in an overloaded airplane, while morbidly obese, having the need for a sleeping aid, and taking an amphetamine that would make sleep more difficult. It is crystal clear this pilot was impaired. His decision making proves that he was.

If you were at all serious about finding out about his impairments, you could always just get a hold of his medical records and his pharmacy records. If you wanted to write comedy, you could say something like, "He was morbidly obese, on uppers, on downers, was flying illegally, and overloaded the airplane while transporting a passenger...but we can't tell if he was impaired." The NTSB just *defined* impairment.

The real question is if there was anything about this decision to turn on the ignition and fly that day that smacks of nonimpairment.

CEN09LA555B AND A

These were two planes involved in a midair collision in Ohio. In this accident, an uncertified pilot flying illegally ran into a certified pilot flying an uncertified aircraft. One of the two persons, neither of whom was flying legally, survived.

MIA08LA138

In this accident, we have some clues about the pilot's health and about his honesty. But there was no serious attempt to figure out whether the pilot lied or didn't lie about his diabetes.

In the NTSB report it stated the following:

The pilot, age 65, held a private pilot certificate, with ratings for airplane single-engine land, airplane single-engine sea, and instrument airplane, issued on May 6, 1981. His third-class medical certificate was issued on July 7, 2008, with a restriction that he must have available glasses for near vision. The pilot reported on his most recent medical certificate that he had accumulated 2,600 total flight hours. The pilot's logbook was not recovered for examination.

The NTSB also reported:

Forensic toxicology was performed on specimens from the pilot by the Federal Aviation Administration (FAA) Bioaeronautical Sciences Research Laboratory, Oklahoma City, Oklahoma. The toxicology report stated that there was no carbon monoxide or cyanide detected in blood, and no ethanol detected in vitreous. However, minoxidil, pioglitazone, and ranitidine were detected in blood and urine.

So what do we know?

The pilot had diabetes, and the pilot may or may not have told his flight examiner this on his medical two days before his accident on July 9, 2008. Or do we even know that? On page four of the NTSB narrative, it stated his last medical was in July 2006. So which is it? Did he start taking diabetes medicines before or after his last medical? This is important, as it shows whether he was honest on his medical. If he wasn't honest, then we need to figure out what else he was willing to lie about besides the most important item on the aircraft: the pilot. It is also important to the pilot's memory, because if everything he did was in good faith and this was simply a clerical error compounded by a lack of sincere effort to get to the facts on this investigation, then his family and his memory deserve to have this information clarified.

MIA08LA161

The next fatal accident allowed the NTSB to clearly state a medical reason for the accident. The toxicology gift wrapped it for them:

To wit:

> Witnesses observed the non-certificated pilot with a passenger on board the unregistered, experimental light sport aircraft. The pilot of the weight-shift trike was performing a low-level maneuver above the bay when the trike made contact with the water and crashed. One witness, a friend of the pilot, reported that the pilot commonly performed the low-level maneuver as a greeting to the local residents in the area. Examination of the wreckage did not reveal any evidence of a preimpact failure or malfunction with the trike and its systems. The postmortem toxicology testing revealed the pilot had a blood alcohol level of 159 mg/dl (0.159 percent). The pilot would have been substantially impaired and may have been alcohol dependent given his apparent tolerance to the sedative effects of alcohol.

Thus, the pilot was flying illegally, in an illegal aircraft, while on alcohol, with a passenger. He died in the process. Thankfully the passenger survived.

ANC09FA003

This accident was a case of hubris meeting incompetency. The sixty-one-year-old pilot was not endorsed by his instructor to solo, and he was in an airplane that wasn't legal to fly, as the instructor stated he would not continue instructing the pilot until the airplane was in compliance and had had its annual exam. Instead, the sixty-one-year-old student chose to fly anyway and quite quickly demonstrated why his instructor felt that he wasn't able to safely solo.

ERA09LA013

One wants to be clear, though. When the NTSB is handed the results of a fatal accident on a silver platter, gift wrapped, sealed, and signed, it does a very good job reporting it. This is one of those accidents.

A pilot bought an airplane he had never flown, got in it with zero hours of instruction, took off, lost control of it, and died. The NTSB cited the following information from his toxicology report, which made it fairly easy for it to decide a probable cause:

> The FAA's Bioaeronautical Sciences Research Laboratory, Oklahoma City, Oklahoma, performed toxicological testing of the pilot. Fluid and tissue specimens from the pilot tested positive for tetrahydrocannabinol (Marijuana) and tramadol, a prescription pain killer.

The NTSB's probable cause:

> The pilot's loss of control in flight due to a lack of flight experience or instruction. Contributing to the accident was the pilot's impairment due to the recent use of marijuana and a prescription painkiller.

When the swiss cheese puts itself on the plate and then lines itself up so that you can see right through it, it makes accident investigations fairly simple.

WPR10LA104

Two people were killed in the next accident. It was another silver-platter event.

Per the NTSB:

HISTORY OF FLIGHT

On January 9, 2010, about 1308 Pacific Standard Time, an experimental weight-shift-control Airborne Streak 2, N155TD, collided with terrain near Lake Isabella, California. The pilot/owner was operating the airplane under the provisions of 14 Code of Federal Regulations (CFR) Part 91. The pilot, who did not possess a pilot certificate, and one passenger were killed; the airplane sustained substantial damage from impact forces. The local personal flight departed at an unknown time. Visual meteorological conditions prevailed, and no flight plan had been filed. Several witnesses observed the airplane flying around during the morning. One described the airplane as buzzing the lake, and performing maneuvers that seemed to be dangerous. Estimates of the altitude varied between 300 and 500 feet above ground level (agl). One of them thought that the engine stopped, and another did not hear the engine. They all reported that they observed one wing folded up. Another witness reported that a neighbor went up with the pilot the day before the accident, and the pilot did not use seat belts.

One witness observed the airplane performing aerobatic maneuvers like a stunt plane all day. The pilot appeared to be attempting to perform loops, and made numerous nose high and nose low maneuvers. The pilot would point the nose toward the ground, and then pull up at the last moment to a high nose up attitude. The witness estimated that the maximum altitude for all of the maneuvers was 300 feet above ground level. He thought that the airplane landed, and then returned and started maneuvering again.

The witness observed the airplane in level flight. The nose went down steeply 45–90 degrees, and then started going up. Just after the nose went above the horizon, the right wing folded up. The engine cut out, and the airplane started down in a free fall and began to spiral. He said that there were no birds or any other objects near the airplane when it went down.

PERSONNEL INFORMATION
A Federal Aviation Administration (FAA) inspector reported that the 31-year-old pilot did not hold a pilot certificate or aviation medical certificate.

This seems almost like the pilot was on drugs!

They established control continuity for all flight controls. The pilot did not appear to be wearing a seat belt; one side of the lap belt was tucked in at the left side of the seat.

MEDICAL AND PATHOLOGICAL INFORMATION
The Kern County Coroner completed an autopsy. The FAA Forensic Toxicology Research Team, Oklahoma City, Oklahoma, performed toxicological testing of specimens of the pilot. They did not perform tests for carbon monoxide or cyanide.

The report contained the following findings for tested drugs: 0.12 (ug/ml, ug/g) amphetamine detected in liver; 0.07 (ug/ml, ug/g) amphetamine detected in kidney; 0.026 (ug/ml, ug/g) diazepam detected in liver; 0.628 (ug/ml, ug/g) methamphetamine detected in liver; 0.408 (ug/ml, ug/g) methamphetamine detected in kidney; 0.064 (ug/ml, ug/g) Nordiazepam detected in liver; 0.037 (ug/ml, ug/g) Nordiazepam detected in kidney; Tetrahydrocannabinol (Marihuana) detected in lung; Tetrahydrocannabinol Carboxylic Acid (Marihuana) detected in lung; Tetrahydrocannabinol Carboxylic Acid (Marihuana) detected in liver; and Tetrahydrocannabinol Carboxylic Acid (Marihuana) detected in kidney.

On a bright note, the NTSB didn't claim the lack of seat belts as the probable cause. Instead it stated:

> Post-mortem toxicology testing on the pilot was consistent with use of methamphetamine, marijuana, and diazepam, but there was no urine or blood available for testing; therefore, it was not possible to estimate the last time when the substances might have been used or whether the pilot may have been impaired by that use. The operating limitations for the airplane noted that it was prohibited from aerobatic flight.

So the fact the pilot was not licensed, didn't wear his seat belts, took a passenger up to do acrobatic maneuvers in a nonacrobatic plane, and had toxicological evidence of two illegal drugs and one prescription sedating drug wasn't enough for the NTSB? The word is *probable*! They were handed the answer on an FAA toxicology report, and they ignored it based on it being liver and kidney and not blood?

Methamphetamine is addictive. Diazepam is addictive. Marijuana is illegal in most states. We have clear evidence that the pilot was on two highly addictive medications, and we supposed to think he had the judgment to stop the medications and put his addictions on hold simply for the thrill of illegally piloting his aircraft without his seat belts in a highly unsafe manner but in as safe an unsafe manner as possible because he safely stopped his illegal medication long enough for it not to impair him prior to him recklessly flying unsafely without a license?

It is almost as if the NTSB needs the same level of drug testing as this pilot did. We are supposed to believe that the one intelligent thing the pilot did on the last day of his life was to decide for a very, very brief moment to make a good decision prior to flying and to *not* take his addicting drugs? And then to fly in a manner that would make the entire world think he was on impairing drugs?

Here we have at least seven factors:

1. An illegal pilot
2. Sedating addictive medications
3. Muscle relaxants
4. Amphetamines
5. Reckless behavior
6. No seat belts during acrobatics in an airplane
7. Death

What is there on that toxicology report that includes his behavior, his certification (none), his usage of amphetamines, sedatives, and marijuana that makes one decide that you can't determine a probability of impairment??

ERA10LA119

Narcotics, a lack of a pilot's license, and generalized arrogance make for a bad flight. In this accident, a fifty-two-year-old pilot without any pilot's license, while on narcotics, decided he would illegally fly. He did for a short period of time. The NTSB report called him a student pilot, but in fact he hadn't had a student pilot's certificate for more than four years, so we have an unregistered airplane, uncertificated pilot, sedating addictive drugs, and no governor on his impulse control. All in all, a pretty clear medical accident. Thankfully no passengers were on board. In a very rare comment in the probable-cause report, the NTSB stated:

The autopsy revealed that the pilot had an active hepatitis C infection with early evidence of liver cirrhosis. It is possible that the pilot was impaired by his recent narcotic use, by symptoms of chronic active hepatitis C infection, or by some other condition for which he was taking the prescription narcotic medication.

It is nice to see that the NTSB can occasionally state this. If it wasn't for the toxicology screening and the autopsy, of course, it would have said nothing at all. It is also a bit ironic to consider that it has a mandate to collect medical history information by law, and yet it stated, "or some other condition," implicitly admitting nobody bothered to look into what other conditions the pilot had.

CEN10LA099B AND A

In this midair accident, a passenger and a pilot in one aircraft were killed. Neither pilot was certificated; both were flying illegally. It really doesn't seem relevant who was at fault in the actual collision, since both were at fault for being in the air illegally. A bigger insult to the passenger's family is if no one bothered to aggressively prosecute the pilot who did survive. One can't learn a lesson if one isn't held to account.

CEN10FA141

In this accident, a light-sport pilot took another person into IMC conditions, killing both of them. The pilot flew a cross-country into weather, apparently not bothering to check conditions thoroughly prior to departure. He was on narcotics and had a host of other issues that the NTSB spelled out. And in this extremely rare instance, it went to the trouble of proving that when it makes an effort, it can approximate its mandate, quite nicely, in fact:

The FAA's Final Forensic Toxicology Fatal Accident Report for the pilot reported the following:
chlorpheniramine detected in lung and kidney, 0.14 (ug/ml, ug/g) hydrocodone detected in lung, 0.089(ug/ml, ug/g) hydrocodone detected in kidney, irbesartan detected in lung and

kidney, phentermine detected in lung and kidney, 0.275 (ug/ml, ug/g) temazepam detected in kidney, and 0.142 (ug/ml, ug/g) temazepam detected in lung.

A review of the pilot's personal medical records indicated a history of multiple medical conditions, including diabetes, kidney disease, high blood pressure, high cholesterol, insomnia, possible obstructive sleep apnea, possible glaucoma, LASIK surgery, cataract surgery, and nasal allergies, among others. Records indicated that medical care had been received by the pilot from a Veterans Affairs (VA) Medical Center, a non-VA primary care physician, a non-VA endocrinologist, a non-VA kidney specialist, and a non-VA ophthalmologist, among others. Records noted the use of multiple medications, including glyburide (5 mg twice a day), sitagliptin (50 mg per day), and exenatide (ten mcg subcutaneously twice a day) for diabetes; niacin (1,000 mg per day) and ezetemibe/simvastatin (10 mg/40 mg per day) for cholesterol, irbesartan/hydrochlorothiazide (300/12.5 mg daily) for high blood pressure; and a prior prescription for temazepam (30 mg) for use at night.

None of the records reviewed indicated any prescriptions for phentermine. The pilot's most recent (as of September 30, 2009) weight was noted as 258 pounds and his height was 71 inches. An exercise stress test performed in January 2006 did not identify any abnormalities.

The medical records also noted that the pilot was seen by a non-VA primary care physician with symptoms of cough and shortness of breath on October, 20, 2009, and a prescription was filled in the pilot's name for an extended release hydrocodone/chlorpheniramine syrup from that physician on October 13, 2009, with refills on December 13, 2009, and on March 4, 2010, the day prior to the accident.

The March 4, 2010, refill of the hydrocodone/chlorpheniramine syrup was found in the wreckage, along with a nasal decongestant spray, a nasal steroid spray, and a separate bottle of over-the-counter chlorpheniramine tablets. The bottle of hy-drocodone/chlorpheniramine syrup was labeled with the brand name (Tussionex) of the compound, and did not note that chlor-pheniramine was a component. Information printed on the back and side of the bottle included: "Shake well before using," "Do not drink alcoholic beverages when taking this medication," "May cause blurred vision," "Taking more than recommended may cause breathing problems," and "May make you drowsy/diz-zy, especially with alcohol. Use care with car-machines."

So let us itemize the causatives that are probable in this accident:

1. Morbid obesity
2. Diabetes
3. Hypertension
4. Sleep apnea
5. Glaucoma
6. Kidney disease
7. Stimulants
8. Sedatives
9. Narcotics
10. Sedating antihistamine

The NTSB has a sense of humor. After all the data collection, all the compilation, all the obvious medical causatives associated with this pilot's decision to fly into well-described IMC conditions that were openly reported to exist and that he didn't bother to check, the NTSB stated the following in its probable-cause report:

The pilot was taking three different medications to treat his diabetes, which would have increased his risk for impairment due to excessively low blood sugar. He had been using a medi-cation for respiratory symptoms combining a narcotic and an antihistamine, both of which have potentially impairing effects. He also may have taken another medication containing the same antihistamine. He had been using a stimulant typically prescribed for weight loss and a sedative previously prescribed for insomnia. He was at high risk for, and had previously been noted to possibly have, obstructive sleep apnea, which can cause severe fatigue and resultant impairment. The pilot may have been impaired or distracted by symptoms of his medical conditions or by effects of medications used to treat those conditions. The extent to which such possible impairment or distraction may have contributed to the accident is unclear. The crash severity precluded the determination of the existence or absence of substantive pre-existing disease, or the determination regarding when medications may have most recently been used.

That is high comedy.

The pilot's choice to fly an aircraft when he knew his medical condition is a sign of a mental illness called delusion. There isn't a probability that he was impaired; it is 100 percent fact he was impaired. The moment he decided to turn on that ignition, that became clear.

This gentleman had no business in an aircraft and had absolutely no business taking up a passenger into known IMC conditions. The travesty is that the NTSB's humor is thrown into the face of an innocent victim.

WPR10LA292

It won't take much for you to guess about the cause of the next light-sport accident:

Take this:

The pilot, age 59, did not hold a pilot certificate or medical certificate. The pilot's son stated that the pilot had flown hang gliders in the 1970s, but had never flown a motorized one before.

The pilot purchased the aircraft on March 19, 2010. The pilot's son indicated that the pilot had not received any instruction in the aircraft, and that this was his first flight.

And this:

Forensic toxicology was performed on specimens from the pilot by the FAA Bioaeronautical Sciences Research Laboratory, Oklahoma City, Oklahoma. The toxicology report stated no ethanol was detected in urine.

The following screened drugs were detected; 0.578 ug/ml 7-amino-clonazepam detected in liver, 7-amino-clonazepam detected in urine, 10.77 ug/ml acetaminophen detected in urine, 1.893 ug/ml codeine detected in urine, 0.144 ug/ml dihydrocodeine detected in urine, 0.326 up/ml hydrocodone detected in urine, 0.325 ug/ml hydromorphone detected in urine, and 3.198 up/ml morphine detected in urine.

So that wasn't hard to figure out, was it? A drugged pilot flying illegally.

WPR10LA462

A seventy-year-old diabetic pilot died in this accident. He was not certified. He also didn't bother to follow the *Pilot's Operating Handbook* for his aircraft. As a result, his airplane took off when he wasn't ready to take off, with a gust lock still in place, leaving him to come along for the ride.

ERA11LA056

In this accident, a noncertificated "pilot" with forty-four illegal hours spun his aircraft and died. His toxicology report helped the investigation along.

To wit:

Forensic toxicology was performed on specimens of the pilot by the FAA Bioaeronautical Sciences Research Laboratory (CAMI), Oklahoma City, Oklahoma, and also the Instituto De Ciencias Forenses, San Juan, Puerto Rico. The toxicology report by CAMI stated the results were negative for carbon monoxide, cyanide, and volatiles. Unquantified amounts of desmethlysertraline, sertraline, and metoprolol were detected in the urine specimen, while an unquantified amount of metoprolol was detected in the cavity blood. Alpha-hydroxyalprazolam (0.216 ug/mL), alprazolam (0.092 ug/mL), Oxazepam (0.031 ug/mL), and temazepam (0.164 ug/mL) were detected in the urine specimen. Desmethlysertraline (0.16 ug/mL) and sertraline (0.172 ug/mL) were detected in the cavity blood, while desmethlysertraline (1.026 ug/mL) and sertraline (0.238 ug/mL) were detected in the heart blood, which was not suitable for analysis for alprazolam. Alpha-hydroxyalprazolam, oxazepam, and temazepam were not detected in the heart blood.

In simple English, there are six factors:

1. Antidepressants
2. A disease that required antidepressants
3. Anti-anxiety medication
4. A disease that required anti-anxiolytics
5. A beta-blocker
6. A disease that would require a beta-blocker

The cause of this crash was that a pilot chose to fly without possessing the certifications or the skill set to do so.

Per the NTSB's probable cause: "The pilot's failure to maintain adequate airspeed, which resulted in an aerodynamic stall and entry into a spin."

That would be a description of the crash, not the cause of it.

CEN11FA480

This was an accident waiting to happen. The pilot had previously been witnessed flying low. This time he died when he spun out, possibly to avoid power lines, which are often found at the altitude at which he utilized his judgment to fly. He began flying at age eighty, and, according to the NTSB report, he had hypothyroidism, a major illness that can cause depression. Depression that was being treated with antidepressants. Atrial fibrillation, a major illness that can cause multiple strokes as well as damage major organs, and Exelon, a medication for Alzheimer's, are also mentioned for some reason.

The NTSB report stated the following:

> According to the autopsy report, the pilot's past medical history was significant for hyperlipidemia, hypothyroidism, depression, and atrial fibrillation. The cause of death was determined to be blunt force injury to the head and chest and the manner of death to be accident. No significant natural disease was identified.

This is probably simply poor English on the NTSB's part, since right after mentioning three major illnesses, it states that no significant disease was identified.

What the poorly written NTSB report seems to be trying to say was the medical examiner who performed the autopsy did a better job looking at the past medical records than the investigators did and looked at the gentleman's past medical records whereas the investigators did not.. A hell of an admission for an organization tasked with fully investigating the causes of accidents while handed the full arsenal of tools to do so. The NTSB knew where the medical records could be found, it listed that the person performing the autopsy had access to these records.

And one additional point. The NTSB uses autopsy and toxicology as a decision tree on whether to go back to sleep and stop bothering to investigate. The autopsy mentioned depression, hypothyroidism, and atrial fibrillation in the medical history. None of those are diseases you would necessarily find looking on an autopsy or a toxicology report.. The NTSB pointed out without seeming to realize it did that an autopsy has a limited role in accident investigation. If it is positive for disease, that is great, but it isn't the end all, be all, it is only a piece of the puzzle, just like a rudder is simply a part of an airplane, and I assume no one would think that if you just looked at the rudder and it was normal you would declare an aircraft had no mechanical defects.

WPR11FA333

In this accident, a pilot took off with the fuel valves closed. The airplane made it to five hundred feet before he and his passenger began to fall to their deaths. He was on lorazepam, an anti-anxiety medication that is sedating and addictive, as well as on two blood pressure medications. No attempt appears to have been made to obtain other medical information on this pilot who, at sixty-six years of age, was eligible for Medicare.

This is important, because lorazepam can affect some people over a longer time period than others. It is important to understand that medications have varying effects upon different people, and thus understanding the necessity of individually assessing a patient's medical history, particularly since the kidneys are vital in the excretion of this drug, and many hypertension patients will have some degree of renal insufficiency. You won't know what you don't know if you don't even bother to look. What we do know is the guy was on anti-anxiety medication and forgot to preflight his airplane properly. That is enough to make me curious.

ERA11LA415

Two people died doing acrobatics in a non-acrobatic airplane. The forty-year-old wasn't even a pilot. According to the NTSB, the aircraft also wasn't registered. Add to that the NTSB stated the alcohol in the criminal's bloodstream probably didn't help his decision making in any regard. This was clearly a medically caused accident. Mental illness, alcohol abuse, take your pick.

CEN12LA203

Let's just read some excerpts and move on.
Per the NTSB:

> On March 24, 2012, at 1824 central daylight time, an amateur built Enbody model GY 201 Minicab, N416FC, impacted terrain in a residential area in Granite Shoals, Texas, shortly after departing from the Sunrise Beach Airport (2KL), Sunrise Beach Village, Texas. The private pilot was fatally injured and the passenger received serious injuries.

And this:

> The pilot, age seventy-four, held a private pilot certificate with a single-engine land rating. The pilot did not hold a current airman medical certificate, nor was he required to hold a medical certificate to operate a light-sport aircraft.

Finally, read this:

> MEDICAL AND PATHOLOGICAL INFORMATION
> An autopsy was performed on the pilot on March 25, 2012, at the Travis County Medical Examiner's Office, Austin, Texas.

The autopsy report indicated that the pilot's remains were soaked in fuel.

Forensic toxicology was performed on specimens from the pilot by the FAA Bioaeronautical Sciences Research Laboratory, located in Oklahoma City, Oklahoma. The test results revealed:

169 (mg/dL, mg/hg) Ethanol detected in Urine

161 (mg/dL, mg/hg) Ethanol detected in Blood

162 (mg/dL, mg/hg) Ethanol detected in Vitreous

15.05 (ug/ml, ug/g) Acetaminophen detected in Urine

Cetirizine NOT detected in Blood

Cetirizine detected in Urine

Citalopram detected in Urine

0.21 (ug/ml, ug/g) Citalopram detected in Blood

Dextromethorphan detected in Blood

Dextromethorphan detected in Urine

Dextrorphan detected in Blood

0.029 (ug/mL, ug/g) Dihydrocodeine detected in Urine

Dihydrocodeine NOT detected in Blood

Gabapentin detected in Urine

Gabapentin NOT detected in Blood

0.031 (ug/ml, ug/g) Hydrocodone detected in Blood

0.185 (ug/ml, ug/g) Hydrocodone detected in Urine

N-Desmethylcitalopram detected in Urine

0.04 (ug/ml, ug/g) N-Desmethylcitalopram detected in Blood

Tramadol detected in Urine

0.724 (ug/mL, ug/g) Tramadol detected in Blood

Ethanol is primarily a social drug with a central nervous system depressant. Ethanol is also an additive in automotive fuel.

N-desmethylcitalopram is a metabolite of Citalopram. Citalopram is a selective serotonin reuptake inhibitor used as an antidepressant and marketed under the brand name Celexa.

Dihydrocodeine is a metabolite of hydrocodone. Hydrocodone is an opioid analgesic prescribed as a Schedule II controlled substance that is commonly marketed under various brand names, including Vicodin, Lortab, and Norco. Hydrocodone may impair mental and physical abilities.

Tramadol is an opioid pain medication that may impair mental and physical abilities.

Dextromethorphan is a nonsedating cough medication.

Cetirizine is a sedating antihistamine used to treat allergy symptoms.

Gabapentin is a prescription medication used to treat chronic or neuropathic pain or to help prevent seizures.

So the pilot was on multiple sedating medications and suffered from pain and/or addiction, depression, and/or neuralgia. What would a seventy-four-year-old's Medicare or VA records tell us about a gentleman who is on multiple narcotics, multiple antidepressants, and also sedating antihistamines?

I don't know what the Medicare records show, because they aren't in the docket. However, more information is in the NTSB docket that mysteriously didn't make it onto the narrative report.

To wit: "The heart had multiple bypass grafts that were widely patent with severe calcific atherosclerosis of the native vessels."

So what do we know?

Per the NTSB, on the last medical the pilot had with the FAA, he didn't report open-heart surgery. Presuming the flight doctor did his or her job and examined his chest properly, this would mean he had had open-heart surgery in the past nine years, and also had begun having severe pain and depression, which isn't uncommon with heart disease. I am going to guess the gentleman had Medicare. It would be of value to find out when his heart surgery was. Above all else, there is the most telling clue of a major problem that no one bothered to address: Why are there no heart medications or anticholesterol medication in this pilot's system? We have a toxicology screen; we know he was on a lot of medications that a sensible person would never take and then fly with. He had arteriosclerosis and had bypass graft surgery. Where is the postsurgical pharmacological treatment of his heart disease? More important, why was the pilot evidently not getting follow-up? Was it cost? Was it dementia? Was there a terminal illness issue? More importantly, did the government just not bother to look at the government's medical records?

CEN12LA307

Arrogance, bravado, and a sense of invincibility sometimes become pathological. The next accident has some interesting tidbits to glean.

Per the NTSB report:

> Several witnesses reported the airplane had passed the departure end of the runway after take-off, when it leveled off about 100 feet above ground level, accelerated, and suddenly made a steep, nearly vertical, nose-up climb. The airplane then banked to the left to turn northbound. While in the left bank the right wing tip came up "very high," the airplane banked and turned even tighter and the airplane suddenly "nose-dived" into the ground.
>
> Several witnesses reported that in the past they had frequently seen the pilot fly by fast at a very low altitude, then pull the nose up steeply, do a sharp turn, and come back flying back in the opposite direction at high speed and low to the ground. Another person who was not a witness reported that he was not surprised that the pilot had an accident because in the past he seemed to enjoy "showing off" for people when he was flying.

So right away, we have a pilot who was known to other pilots to be a bit over the top. Let's see what else is there.

Per the NTSB: "The pilot, age forty-two, did not hold a currently valid pilot certificate." The following additional findings were noted:

0.059 (ug/ml, ug/g) Amphetamine detected in Urine

0.121 (ug/ml, ug/g) Methamphetamine detected in Urine

0.007 (ug/ml, ug/g) Methamphetamine detected in Blood

OK, moving on. No, wait, the NTSB had one final little thing to say. I almost left it out: "It is unknown whether the pilot was being medically treated for any of those conditions because the investigator-in-charge was not able to contact any of the pilot's medical providers or to examine the pilot's medical records."

What is my issue with this statement? There is absolutely zero evidence that the NTSB routinely makes any attempt whatsoever to find out who the pilots' treating physicians are, even when handed the names via hospital records or FAA past medical exams. If the records were routinely found in the dockets of other accidents, it would be believable. When medical records are almost never found in NTSB dockets, I find this comment to be laughable.

OK, but Dr. Shewmaker, aren't you being harsh? Let's test that theory. The toxicology report gives the gentleman's name. The FAA gives his date of birth on his previous medical exams, but that isn't printed in the NTSB report. Let's start digging a bit. We don't have the date of birth, so let's just look up his obituary in the local paper and go from there. Clock starts now.

In less than one minute on the Internet, I found out his date of birth, where he worked (he was a business owner), and what town he lived in. Using that information, I can guarantee you that with four phone calls I could likely have his medical information by tomorrow afternoon (it's Sunday).

The pilot owned a business. When you own a relatively large business, you often provide health insurance, including for yourself. This can be subpoenaed, but it isn't necessary—you can call up a person working at that business and ask a simple set of questions.

"Are you guys hiring? No? OK, because a friend of mine said you guys did pretty well there. If you do start hiring soon, can I leave you a number or come in and fill out a résumé? Oh, by the way, do you provide health insurance?"

And that is all it would take. You then subpoena the insurance company records, and you will then have all his medical records. This isn't difficult. You just have to care.

The accident happened in a town called Checotah. It has a population of about thirty-five hundred people. Finding the doctors who work there in family practice took me about four more minutes.

Just highlight Checotah, right click, Google search, and look for doctors. Four records request forms, and then twiddle your thumbs until the records arrive. This really isn't all that difficult. My guess is Checotah wasn't an exotic enough locale to warrant spending the time going there and getting to the truth. Illegal or legal amphetamines? We don't know, because we haven't had a thorough accident investigation yet.

15

CLUES TO JUDGMENT

SOME ACCIDENTS GIVE you hints at where to begin an investigation if you truly desire answers. These next examples certainly hint at decision making as a place to begin looking. If the NTSB does adopt a policy of truly investigating general-aviation fatal accidents, it could start by assessing the pilot's normal judgment and choices.

ERA09FA141

This one occurred when the pilot didn't fully preflight his aircraft and, as a result, a passenger died. The pilot appears to have thought another person had connected his aileron controls and not only didn't do a full walk-around to ensure airplane safety of flight; he didn't do a pretakeoff controls check either. This negligence resulted in a death. No survey of this pilot's medical history appears to have been attempted.

ERA09LA150

This accident involved an experienced pilot, with no reported medical issues, who wrecked and died in an aircraft he had just bought and in which he had flown only one hour. The importance of having a flight instructor check you out in an airplane before you try to fly it can't be overstated.

ERA09LA193

In this accident, a pilot with eighteen hours in the previous nine years took a passenger to their death in an airplane he had neglected to register appropriately with the FAA under the new light-sport category. His last medical was expired, and his last flight review was twenty-four months previously. Although he survived for several days in the hospital, no attempt seems to have been made to obtain his full medical records. The NTSB was unable to ascertain a reason for the wreck having occurred. The fact that the pilot appears to have listed no flight time after his last flight review seems to indicate he was either very lax in his recording or he took up a passenger when he wasn't competent to do so.

CEN09FA243

This is an accident where witnesses stated the aircraft seemed to have mechanical issues prior to the crash.

The probable-cause report stated, "The pilot's failure to execute an immediate forced landing to a suitable field and the engine's partial loss of power for an undetermined reason."

The pilot and passenger were killed. The NTSB report faults the pilot's judgment as partially causing these two deaths. The toxicology report was also mentioned in the NTSB report and clearly shows the NTSB has no idea what a toxicology report is telling it.

Per the NTSB:

Toxicology results were consistent with use of Bupropion, a prescription antidepressant also used for smoking cessation. The medication does not impair flying performance, and though there is an increased risk of seizures with the medication, the circumstances of the accident were not consistent with a seizure event.

OK, what did they miss?

Bupropion itself may not have caused a seizure, but it is also used to treat depression. And if the pilot suffered from major depression, then his overall mind-set, judgment, and ability to think clearly could be markedly impacted. Some depressed individuals also have psychotic episodes. To make the statement that a medication prescribed can cause seizures and then claim the event wasn't consistent with a seizure misses the point. The NTSB claimed the pilot had flawed judgment in not immediately landing. The pilot was taking a medication often prescribed to people with a disease that can severely impact judgment.

In fact, many of the people who take antidepressants have already attempted suicide. Not digging into why the pilot was on an antidepressant to see what his physician had previously documented about his thought process and frame of mind indicates the NTSB is ill equipped to understand anything at all about depression and its impact on flying. In *Murder in a 172*, we showed that in Cessna 172s, more than one in twenty fatal accidents are suicides. If anything, the NTSB should have a better handle on suicides and depression than mechanical issues, because suicides appear to kill at least as many pilots as mechanical issues do.

CEN09LA255

In this accident, a pilot with zero hours in the make and model of the aircraft bought an out-of-annual airplane on an "as is" basis, took off to ferry it home, and wrecked, killing himself. The seller didn't seem overly distraught about the situation, as he told the accident investigators that it was an understood agreement that it was "as is, where is."

The pilot who died hadn't flown in more than a year and was a student. The last inspection on the aircraft was more than two and a half years prior. I'd like to think if I were selling an airplane, I would have enough self-respect to make sure the buyer had the mental capacity not to kill himself while the plane was still in my home airstrip's airspace. Perhaps the pilot lied and told the seller he had thousands of hours in type and thus...

ANC09FA062

Two people died in this accident, and they did so in an overloaded airplane. They were going on a fishing trip. The passenger was also giving the pilot a checkout ride, as he was an FAA employee, and the owner of the aircraft was a designated pilot examiner. The probable cause of the accident was they overloaded the aircraft.

The airplane doesn't care how many hours you have, how many type ratings you have, or who employs you. The airplane demands your current competency and attention to detail, every flight, every time.

ERA09LA502

In this accident, a pilot bought an airplane that wasn't airworthy. He wasn't qualified to work on the airplane, yet he did so anyway. The airplane wasn't mechanically sound, yet he took another passenger up for a flight, and two people died.

At some point during the flight, the gearbox and propeller broke away and sheared off the tail of the airplane. The bill of sale from when the pilot bought the aircraft indicated that it wasn't airworthy.

CEN10LA041

Instrument meteorological conditions prevailed. Might as well get right to the details of how a light-sport aircraft that isn't eligible to fly into IMC ends up killing a passenger by flying into IMC.

1. The report stated the accident occurred at 8:00 a.m.
2. The report stated the airplane took off at 7:55 a.m.
3. The report stated witnesses said the airplane was flying at about one hundred feet and went into fog.
4. The pilot, fifty-seven, was not instrument rated.
5. "Witnesses at the accident scene reported fog and clouds lower than 100 feet AGL. One witness describing the fog said, 'It was really foggy; we wondered how the pilot could see.' Another witness said it was very foggy, but he 'could see across the street.'"

So to put this in perspective: a fifty-seven-year-old man put a passenger into his airplane, taxied out to the runway in foggy conditions, knew he was not instrument rated, and took the passenger to his death.

Toxicology and autopsy reports are not sufficient to diagnose pathological judgment, and the hormone for excessive arrogance hasn't been discovered. This was a medical/judgment-related accident. No person with eight hundred hours in aviation who was sufficiently in possession of his mental faculties would have taken a passenger up in such conditions. Make your arguments to the opposite; deafness is a medical condition.

ANC10FA022

The elements of poor decision making are in the next accident, but they are incomplete. The pilot hadn't flown in several months and was taking ibuprofen and Tylenol, but we have no evidence that anyone bothered to figure out why he pitched up his aircraft and lost control. Overall, there isn't much to see here, so move on to the next fatal accident, the public won't notice if this accident was thoroughly investigated.

WPR10FA211

In this accident, a pilot/owner declined to install a parachute in his aircraft but advertised that he used a safety parachute. He lured an unsuspecting customer to buy a birthday flight for a passenger. He flew the airplane in an unsafe manner and lost control, killing himself and the passenger. I'd call that pathologically bad judgment.

WPR10LA293

In this example, a pilot killed himself and his passenger when he tried to maneuver to land. He induced a stall when he attempted a steeper-than-normal turn while flying with both of the airplane doors removed. The increased drag and the steep maneuver were enough to cause the airplane to stall, killing both occupants.

CEN10LA401

First time flying the plane strikes again on this next accident. The pilot hadn't flown for several decades and was getting back into it by building and flying a Zenith at age seventy-four. His last recorded flight prior to his five hours in the six months before he killed himself was in 1984 at the age of forty-eight.

Per the NTSB:

> The pilot's flight instructor stated the pilot stopped flying a number of years ago and she was giving him recurrent training in preparation for a flight review so he could exercise sport pilot privileges. She stated they flew a Cessna 152 and they spoke about the differences between that airplane and the Zenith 701 that the pilot had just built. She stated the pilot did a lot of research and they discussed the 701s "...supposed inability of the elevator to work at slow airspeed without the propwash when the RPMs are pulled back." She stated that because of this characteristic, they practiced stalls and landings using a higher than normal power setting. The Zenith factory was contacted and there was no record that the pilot had flown in a CH701 when

he visited the factory. No evidence was found to indicate the pilot had ever flown a Zenith CH701 aircraft prior to the accident.

The investigator didn't get any medical reports, although there was a beta-blocker in the toxicology report. The autopsy and the toxicology reports are ill equipped to test for levels of judgment. For that we have to look at the actions of the pilot flying illegally in an airplane for which he had received absolutely no instruction, when he had only five hours in the past twenty-six years and wasn't signed off with a current biennial review. I'd say that toxic levels of hubris were present.

A note: if you think I am being unduly harsh and snarky, please remind yourself that innocent people are killed by people such as this. People who clearly lack good decision-making skills and who, by virtue of an overweening need by the government to be accommodating, are allowed to fly with just the OK of the DMV from their states—the same DMV you laugh at.

ERA10LA431

In this light-sport accident, the seventy-one-year-old pilot taxied three-fourths of the way across a lake and then turned back into the wind and attempted to take off. He ran out of room, banked too sharply, spun, and died. Other than blood pressure medicine listed on the toxicology screening, we have no idea what preexisting issues the pilot may have had. He was quite possibly eligible for Medicare, the US government insurance, however, there is no evidence the US government (NTSB) asked itself (Medicare) anything regarding his past medical history

CEN11FA304

This accident killed two persons. The pilot was giving demo flights and took up a person into heavy gusting winds, stalled, and crashed, killing both of them. The toxicology report was negative; however, there is a bit of a clue given. The gentleman had nine thousand flight hours and was type rated in several large aircraft. A video showed him stall the aircraft. Witnesses claimed he flew dangerously. His friends claimed the witnesses had hidden interests in discrediting his memory and that while he often pushed the envelope, he was a very safe pilot. I am still scratching my head at the idea of them defending their friend by claiming he was a very safe pilot who often pushed the envelope. It is in the NTSB docket reports, not the narrative reports.

According to one of his friends, who was rebutting witnesses, "He was a 'Good Stick' and while he was known to occasionally push both himself and his aircraft to their respectable limits, he had the experience and skills to do so and I never knew him to deliberately or recklessly endanger the lives of others in any venue, especially pertaining to flight."

According to another friend:

> With that said, while I've no idea of the onboard fuel load, and weight of Mr. Mcintosh at the time of the accident, I'm sure they were within the aerodynamic envelope, useful load, and weight and balance specifications of the aircraft. Pete pushed the envelope at times (asked an airplane to do what it was designed to do), but there is no way he would have intentionally or knowingly jeopardized the safety of his passenger. Let alone his own! If there was nothing medical or mechanical, then it had to be *severe wind shear* coupled with the attitude of the airplane that caused it to stall and spin.

With friends like that!

The use of the terminology "pushed the envelope at times" is suggestive of a pilot who even his grieving friends knew would put the airplane on the edge of its performance window. Sometimes the Flying Wallendas fell off the wire. It is up to professional risk-takers not to take some innocent to the grave with them. That is called breaking the envelope, not pushing it.

Suffice it to say that if you push the envelope sometimes, according to your dear friends who have a bias toward you, you are more than likely exceeding normal behavior in the minds of most other folk. I'll call this one nonmedical, but was it? Someone made the judgment to fly that gusty day. And two people died because of that poor judgment.

ERA11FA287

In this accident, a pilot attempted to fly a plane at night from Florida to Illinois after flying down earlier that day commercially. The airplane wasn't certified to fly at night. It is speculated that the canopy opened, the pilot attempted to close it, lost control, and crashed. None of that is the real issue. The real big issue is that a pilot who was likely fatigued decided to take a daytime airplane on a long nighttime ride. This is the decision making that led to his death.

WPR11FA225

Two people died in this crash when the pilot lost control while maneuvering over the ocean and cliffs of Hawaii. The airplane was overloaded; the wing had had several patches placed in it and was found to be in a deteriorated, weakened condition. Despite this and the fact that the pilot had contacted persons regarding buying a new wing, he continued to fly, alleging he was doing "flight instruction." This was a medical/judgment-related accident. You have a certain amount of responsibility to do your job. It isn't just the NTSB; pilots also have this responsibility. A pattern of not doing your job or of shoddy performance is evidence of a deeper pathology. In case you missed it, that dart was aimed at two targets.

ERA11LA427

There is no real excuse for this accident, other than hubris and arrogance. Birds don't try to fly through ice, and humans shouldn't violate the laws of physics or the tenets of basic aviation safety and training.

A pilot failed to properly and safely perform a weight and balance, and took up a 340-pound pilot in an aircraft he also did not properly inspect and preflight. Additionally, he later admitted to the NTSB that he didn't know how to actually ensure the emergency parachute was properly prepped and ready for deployment and thus left it in the safety pin, preventing its use. The diabetic student, who was a licensed pilot who hadn't flown for years, had severe coronary artery disease and was wearing a cast.

It didn't help that his weight and girth would have made reaching the deployment handle of the parachute nearly impossible anyway. Overall, this was an accident that didn't have to happen—the pilot used pathologically poor judgment and placed both himself and his passenger into an unsafe situation.

Now, let us consider if the seventy-one-year-old diabetic passenger with severe heart disease who was wearing a cast and weighed 340 pounds had not died and the airplane had somehow made it safely back that day. This diabetic pilot with 1,600 hours, who hadn't flown for years, would likely have then taken one of his family members up for a nice sightseeing trip, and we'd be reading about that accident instead of this one. This isn't the time for nicety and political correctness: a morbidly obese, elderly man with severe diabetes and heart disease has no business endangering others with his hobbies and lifestyle choices.

WPR12FA203

The probable cause of this accident was listed as the pilot's decision to fly low in heavy winds. The toxicology was negative. There was one sentence in an interview with an acquaintance of the pilot that stood out to me. There was no exploration of what the interviewee meant when he said of the deceased pilot, "He and the other club pilots considered the pilot accomplished and nearly 'invincible'—the pilot had 'more than nine lives.'"

I would think this would have opened up Pandora's box. Instead, the report went no further, even when the same interviewer later noted, "Regarding weather information, the pilot 'wasn't one to check ahead.'"

Based on this acquaintance's statements, I'd say we are at the beginning of an accident investigation, not the end of it. The NTSB disagreed, called it pilot error, closed the book, and moved to the next dead light sport pilot.

ERA11FA435

Judgment? Mental illness? Take your pick.

> The pilot, age 70, held a private pilot certificate. According to the pilot's logbook, his last recorded flight was on August 14, 2005. A family member stated that the pilot's wife had urged him to get some flight instruction prior to flying the airplane by himself, since it had been some time since he had flown; however, the pilot declined to do so. The pilot's latest medical certificate was issued on June 6, 2005, and at the time, he indicated 640 hours of flight time.

Well, at least the airplane was safe, right?

> The two-seat airplane was powered by a Rotax 503 engine. According to supporting documentation, the airplane was purchased during an online auction on July 12, 2011, and a bill of sale was signed for it on July 14, 2011. After transport, the airplane was reassembled on the pilot's property. No maintenance logbooks were located; however, the advertisement for sale stated that it had approximately 200 hours of total airframe and engine time, that it had always been hangared, and that it had previously flown under an "ultralight instructor exemption."
>
> An autopsy was conducted on the pilot at the Tennessee Office of the Medical Examiner, Nashville, Tennessee, where the cause of death was determined to be "multiple blunt force

injuries." Subsequent toxicological testing was performed by the FAA Forensic Toxicology Research Team, Oklahoma City, Oklahoma, with the following results: Amlodipine in blood and urine, diphenhydramine in blood and urine, and rosuvastatin in urine only.

The lack of a real attempt to figure out his medical history and, most important, whether he suffered from dementia or other brain disorders is troubling. This seems to be a case of mental skills not being elevated sufficiently to make safe aviation decisions. A seventy-year-old likely has some Medicare or VA records that even the laziest investigator could find.

The ironic backhand slap at the FAA and the EAA and the AOPA and the other proponents of allowing the light-sport class of aircraft can't be escaped. In the docket for this accident is an interview with a witness who was the daughter of the pilot's wife:

> Ms. Pittenger stated that her mother (the pilot's wife) had urged the pilot to obtain instruction in the airplane prior to flying it by himself since it had been some time since he had flown, but the pilot stated that flying was "just like riding a bike." The pilot had also stated that flying this airplane did not require a license or medical certificate.

Just like riding a bike. Off a cliff.

Really, does it get more ironic, the last words of a light-sport pilot, starting up flying simply because the DMV makes no real attempt to figure out whether he should even be driving. It's a hell of an epitaph but one that will await commonsense government decision making before it fits on the light-sport headstone. I am not going to hold my breath.

One only wishes he'd first tried to prove he could still ride a bike. I have my doubts.

CEN11FA645

A twenty-one-year-old pilot and his passenger died in this accident. They were flying low and doing maneuvers over houses when they lost control. Luckily no one else was killed. No evidence of mental illness was included or excluded, although the decision to fly low and perform maneuvers over a congested area does give us a hint why such information might be elucidative. A passenger was killed; I'd like to see this twenty-one-year-old's school and pediatric medical history. ADD? Schizophrenia? Personality disorder? Can't be that hard to dig into. The aircraft departed from Purdue University, so I know where I could probably get his high school transcripts and probably his vaccination records, which quite often provide the pediatrician's address.

WPR13LA347

In this accident, a gentleman, age sixty-five, lost control of his aircraft and crashed. He was on a blood pressure medication and, per a witness who was an instructor, may not have latched his seat belt, performed a preflight without a checklist, and left his car door open before going off to fly.

Medical records and mental-health records were not obtained. Certainly the pilot seems distracted, perhaps in a rush (per the instructor), but there isn't clear evidence for or against a medical cause. There is definitely clear evidence that something might have been lurking under the surface. The investigator knew this as well. Why would you bother to type that a car door was left open and that a gentleman was in a hurry if you didn't think those elements were pertinent? I love nuance and all, but you have to recognize that nuance means "dig deeper," not go, "Hmm, OK, we are done here."

ERA12LA364

In this example, the pilot, age forty-five, lost control of the aircraft and crashed with no determination by the NTSB of cause. The NTSB cited the autopsy as negative for a coronary event. The pilot was on an antihypertensive medication, losartan. The NTSB didn't mention any limitation on finding medical records. It also didn't mention any attempt to get records from the person who would have prescribed the losartan. Trenton, Georgia, has a population of twenty-three hundred or so, with about four doctors in the town.

CEN12LA340

Per the NTSB, the fifty-five-year-old pilot died as a result of inadvertently stalling while maneuvering at a low altitude. The toxicology report was negative. Masonville, Iowa, has a population of about 127. The county seat, Manchester, has a population of about five thousand. No medical records were obtained—or mentioned.

CEN13LA034

In this accident, two people died when they were flying at low altitude, climbed to avoid power lines, and lost control. No medical records were obtained, and the toxicology report on the fifty-two-year-old pilot was negative.

WPR13FA036

Two more persons died when a thirty-nine-year-old student lost control of the aircraft during a flight. The instructor pilot, who was also killed, sat behind the student in the aft seat, which had no controls. Negative toxicology screening and a lack of medical records make this accident investigation incomplete. The NTSB simply reported the airplane probably lost control after inadvertently entering into a spin.

Wash hands; move on to the next accident.

CEN13LA062

In this accident, a sixty-year-old student pilot died when the airplane lost control during an aborted landing.

Per the NTSB: "The pilot's failure to maintain adequate airspeed during initial climb following an aborted landing, which resulted in an aerodynamic stall and spin at a low altitude."

Negative toxicology, negative medical record assessment.

CEN14LA243

In this accident, a pilot lost control and crashed. The toxicology was negative, and after an "exhaustive" yearlong investigation involving printing out the aircraft certification documentation and discussing the accident briefly, little else appears to have been found—or looked for. Left off the narrative was one important detail regarding the seventy-two-year-old pilot's loss of control. It was in the interview with the FAA inspectors:

> They noted that they could find no record of the airplane having received a condition inspection for several years. They noted that the airplane was flying at low altitude and believed to be circling the home of a friend of the pilot before crashing.

The seventy-two-year-old man, who was a retired military officer, likely had government medical insurance. The government branch tasked by law with fully investigating aviation accidents didn't attempt to obtain medical records from the government. All we are left with is a pilot age seventy-two, wrecked in an airplane that likely wasn't being properly maintained, while likely flying dangerously.

The aircraft instruments weren't even capable of reading the speed at which the aircraft would have stalled.

Per the probable cause report:

> The pilot's failure to maintain adequate airspeed and his exceedance of the airplane's critical angle-of-attack while maneuvering

at low altitude, which led to an aerodynamic stall and loss of control. Contributing to the accident was the installation of an inappropriate airspeed indicator that did not provide airspeed indications near the airplane's stall speed.

A sane person doesn't do insane things. And insane people can hardly self-certify to their abilities.

CEN14LA379

The next accident was the case of a pilot without a pilot's certificate flying low to obtain GoPro pictures. He died.

Narrative 1:

During a telephone conversation Sheriff Kelly stated the following: Sheriff Kelly was in his yard with his son. They heard what sounded like an ultralight airplane make a low pass. They looked and observed a small airplane make a turn and eventually lost sight of the airplane as it disappeared behind the trees, flying over Wallace Lake. The airplane came back up over the trees at which time they heard the engine of the airplane rev several times.

It sounded like the pilot was increasing power to the engine in attempt to climb. The airplane descended toward the trees and they heard a "boom" or "thud" like something heavy was dropped on the ground.

Sheriff Kelly and his son immediately went to the airplane. He stated that there was fuel in the fuel tank and that no fuel was leaking from the airplane. He stated that a GoPro Camera was attached to the airplane and the airplane was damaged by the impact. He stated that the pilot was known in the area as a wildlife photographer.

Narrative 2:

During conversations with Inspector Benedetto, he stated the following:

One witness, the Sheriff, lived close to the accident location. He observed the airplane flying over the lake and then make a turn toward him. He lost sight of the airplane due to the trees. Shortly thereafter he heard the airplane crash but did not see the impact.

The owner of the airplane stated that the pilot was taking aerial photographs of some land that the owner was interested in purchasing. The airplane met the requirements for a light sport airplane. The airplane did not have an "N" number and was never registered with the FAA. Inspector Benedetto stated that the owner of the airplane, Mr. Keeth, purchased the airplane a year ago. The previous owner told Mr. Keeth that it was experimental and if there were two people on board he would have to register it. There were no maintenance records for the airplane.

The airplane appeared to have struck the tree before hitting the ground. The flight controls were continuous and the engine and propeller assembly remained attached to the airframe. Both wings were bent and wrinkled, the fuselage was crushed, and the windscreen and instrument panel were broken. He stated that the propeller was damaged but remained attached to the engine. The inspector stated that there were no mechanical anomalies with the airplane or the engine that would have precluded normal operation. The pilot did not hold any pilot certificate or airman medical certificate.

That was the entire text that is listed on the docket.

Two phone interviews and five pictures of a crumpled airplane were all that was included in the docket.

In fairness, it isn't possible from the rudimentary evidence to say whether the GoPro was the only camera the illegally flying pilot was using to take pictures. Unlike another accident where the pilot actually had a camera around his neck and the last photo coincided almost precisely with his loss of control.

16

THE FINAL PARADOXES

THE CONCEPT OF self-certification presumes a cognitive skill set that is above a certain minimal level. It is clear from this book thus far that some pilots do not possess that skill. This is the reason we have to seriously consider the nonsensical concept of allowing people to fly simply because the DMV refuses to do its job and lets anyone and their 103-year-old mother onto a highway she thinks is lined with unicorns. The whole concept of the light-sport class and doing away with medical examinations for pilots is simply silly.

This paradox, wherein a person with no judgment is asked to determine whether she has a grounding condition, plays itself out so often that we can't ignore it. Routine monitoring by an objective person is required. It needs to be thorough, and it needs to be more focused on the judgment and decisions a pilot must make prior to flying.

The arrogant pilot who sees nothing wrong with taking people to their deaths while the pilot is drugged, sedated, or severely ill is the last person who should be placed into a system without proper checks and balances.

Further, we have a paradox wherein an agency tasked with investigating aviation accidents sits on its thumbs until the very rare major accident kills several hundred people. The agency's employees descend en masse on this high-publicity event and then crawl back into their cubicles to pay lip service to accidents in the general-aviation community that have killed far more pilots and passengers. They publish these marginally investigated findings into "probable-cause" reports that patently demonstrate an ignorance of the definition of *probable.*

The "aviation safety" experts in the various pilot groups then use these "probable-cause" reports to tell the public that judgment and medical issues aren't that big a deal in general aviation. They do this because they don't realize the NTSB reports are shoddy, or they ignore the shoddiness because it fits their narrative of creating less oversight, or both.

Here are examples of these paradoxes.

ERA12FA006

Occasionally the NTSB surprises me. This seventy-year-old gentleman died in an airplane he had built himself. So we need to know if he was mentally and physically capable of building an airplane, as well as mentally and physically capable of flying said airplane. The airplane crashed. Let's start with the accident report:

> Forensic toxicology was performed on specimens from the pilot by the FAA Bioaeronautical Sciences Research Laboratory, Oklahoma City, Oklahoma. The toxicology reported stated Amlodipine was detected in the liver and the blood, Etomidate was detected in the liver; 0.101 (ug/mL, ug/g) Midazolam was detected in the liver; however, neither Etomidate nor Midazolam were detected in the blood.
>
> Review of the pilot's personal medical records by an NTSB medical officer revealed a diagnosis of hypertension and Amlodipine (marketed under the trade name Norvasc) is a medication used to treat hypertension. Etomidate is an anesthesia induction agent and Midazolam is a benzodiazepine commonly

used for sedation during medical procedures; both of which are only available in intravenous formulations and were documented as being administered during the hospital resuscitation.

Trauma medical records also included documentation of the pilot's usual medication. Those listed medications were used to treat hypertension, decrease the heart's work in moderate to severe congestive heart failure, as well as other medications that treat and prevent life-threatening, recurrent ventricular arrhythmias and also used to treat atrial fibrillation.

During the autopsy an indwelling medical device was removed and sent to the manufacturer for readout. There was no evidence of a tachyarrhythmia or defibrillation being recorded. The autopsy also revealed that the heart was enlarged overall and a "bulging left ventricle" with left ventricular hypertrophy.

There was evidence of minimal coronary artery disease; however, the lateral aspect of the left ventricle has a 3.0 cm area of interstitial fibrosis was consistent with a remote heart attack. Review of the indwelling medical device manufacturer's records showed a previous pacemaker had been exchanged for a combination pacemaker/automated internal cardiac defibrillator about eight months prior to the accident. For further information please refer to the "Medical Factual" report located in the docket associated with this accident.

This pilot had congestive heart failure, a previous heart attack, arrhythmia, a pacemaker, and a defibrillator. OK, that sounds like a perfectly fine situation..

Also, evidently the previous pacemaker wasn't doing a good enough job controlling the pilot's heart, so it was exchanged for a defibrillator/pacemaker so that when the pilot went into an arrhythmia and approached death, the defibrillator would administer an electrical shock to his heart and basically pound it like a hammer to get it electrically restarted.

And:

> According to CFR 61.53(b) "Prohibition on operations during medical deficiency" states in part "...Operations that do not require a medical certificate...a person shall not act as pilot in command, or in any other capacity as a required pilot flight crewmember, while that person knows or has reason to know of any medical condition that would make the person unable to operate the aircraft in a safe manner."

If this gentleman didn't know that he had a deficiency that made him unable to operate an aircraft in a safe manner, then heart disease wasn't his only issue; mental cognition was also totally lacking.

This is the essence of the problem played out in real life with the light-sport class. The FAA uses government doublespeak to say you can fly using your DMV-vetted driver's license. But you can't fly if *you* know of any medical condition that prevents you from flying.

So legally, a mentally ill person with dementia and a driver's license is good to fly, because he has no mental capacity to self-assess. It is a blatantly idiotic paradox. A demented person *can't* know or have reason to know he is demented by definition.

The medical report from the NTSB starts with the following:

> The following were reviewed by the Chief Medical Officer for the National Transportation Safety Board, Mary Pat McKay, MD, MPH: the FAA blue ribbon medical file, records from the pilot's postcrash emergency care, the autopsy and toxicology findings, and the results from interrogation of the pilot's indwelling cardiac device.

OK then. But let's go back to a previous narrative report on a medically related fatal accident in which the lymphoma/diabetes/heart-diseased pilot died of a fatal heart issue.

ERA11LA496

"The pilot applied for another third-class medical certificate on May 9, 2011; however, the medical application was deferred for review due to a history of coronary artery disease, hypertension, lymphoma, and diabetes."

In this accident, the NTSB apparently made no attempt to obtain this pilot's "blue ribbon" FAA records. If you are going to investigate accidents, you need to have a protocol. "Sometimes do, sometimes don't" isn't going to get you to your goal.

It isn't as if the NTSB doesn't know about checklists. On a lot of accident reports, it mentions that a pilot didn't use the pilot checklist properly. It just seems it has never realized that a checklist of medical items it needs to gather prior to finishing an investigation might serve it in the same manner that it would have served the pilots it criticizes for not utilizing such a tool. Irony.

May I suggest using the following boilerplate comment?

"We, the NTSB, find that you, the pilot, didn't use your checklist properly and took off with flaps improperly set. Unfortunately, since we have no checklist for assessing human factors, we can't tell whether your improper use of a checklist was medical due to our lack of possessing a checklist to make such a determination."

ERA12FA006 and ERA11LA496 occurred eighteen days apart. One listed FAA medical records but didn't obtain them. The other mentioned an indwelling pacemaker/defibrillator, and the NTSB light bulb went off: "Hey, let's get FAA records." Both fatal accidents. Both with obvious medical issues. One: get his FAA records. Two: ignore that the FAA is telling us they have a ton of the pilot's medical records. It is scary, strange, and frankly pathetic. It shows a lack of a system.

Are we seeing a problem here yet?

Even though the NTSB obtained the pilot's (the one with the defibrillator) FAA and hospital records, it didn't take the obvious next step and get his primary-care and cardiologist records. It took the first step, though, and that is a promising and pleasant rarity.

WPR12FA395

In this accident, the eighty-one-year-old pilot was "flying up to his ranch property to check on cattle."

Aside from two blood pressure medications found in the toxicology report, there is absolutely no evidence any attempt to look at medical factors was made. Idaho doesn't have good off-Broadway shows, and the media doesn't flock around the high chaparral like it will the East River.

The pilot's failure to maintain adequate airspeed while maneuvering at or above the airplane's maximum ceiling resulted in a stall and a subsequent loss of airplane control. Contributing to the accident was the pilot's decision to operate the airplane in high-density altitude conditions, which placed the airplane near or above its maximum ceiling.

You have a pilot-error accident due to both planning and operational mistakes. That would indicate a need to rule out any dementia, mental illness, or other neurological issues. These often aren't going to find their way onto a toxicology screen. You figured out the density altitude and the fact that the pilot shouldn't have gone flying. So why did the pilot go flying? Take the next step.

CEN12LA634

The importance of getting medical records becomes crystal clear when you consider that in the next narrative report, the NTSB did actually obtain medical history. Again, in this case, from the wife of the deceased pilot rather than from a more thorough review of medical records, but it will make a major point.

The report stated:

> During the post-accident investigation, the NTSB Investigator-In-Charge and a FAA Medical Officer interviewed the pilot's spouse to ascertain the pilot's previous medical history. The pilot had an artificial aortic heart valve replacement for the past thirty-eight years and was on a daily regimen of Coumadin.

Additionally, he had coagulation studies done monthly, which were reportedly normal and there were no known issues with his replacement heart valve. The pilot had heart bypass surgery in the 1990s. In 2006 he had a cardiac catheterization to evaluate ischemia and to install a stent in an artery that was 90 percent occluded; however, the location of the occlusion prevented stenting and his previous surgeries prevented additional surgical intervention. The pilot was reportedly receiving medical treatment for his ischemic coronary artery disease.

The pilot had a craniotomy after developing slurred speech resulting from a slowly expanding subdural hematoma sustained during a ski accident about ten years before his fatal aviation accident. Following the craniotomy, his slurred speech resolved and he had no residual neurological symptoms.

The pilot's spouse reported that the pilot had four or five episodes of transient ischemic attack; however, the symptoms of each episode were always different. More than ten years before the accident flight and before his craniotomy surgery, the pilot experienced double vision while driving. Then about a year later he had another episode when he told his wife that he was experiencing eye problems and his wife noted that his eyes were bulging; however, the symptoms resolved after a few seconds. Since his craniotomy procedure, while operating an automobile, the pilot reportedly lost vision and had to pull over and let his wife drive. The final episode occurred three or four years before the accident flight, when the pilot told his wife that he felt the table was tipping, but she noted he was leaning instead.

The pilot's spouse reported that each episode lasted only a few seconds and after which, the pilot exhibited no residual symptoms. Following his most recent episode, which occurred three to four years before the accident flight, the pilot's spouse asked her husband to tell his physician about his latest episode; however, she did not know if he indeed told his doctor or not.

The pilot was evaluated by his personal physician in February 2008 and was diagnosed with dizziness and counseled him against driving or flying. However, records show that in April 2010, the pilot passed an exam for a commercial driver's license.

Now for the eight major points:

1. Did the pilot lie on his exam for a commercial license?
2. He had had repeated blood clots impacting blood vessels in his brain—that is the definition of multiple TIAs.
3. He had severe coronary artery disease, partially revascularized and beyond further surgical repair.
4. He had visual issues.
5. He had dizziness.
6. He'd had heart valve replacement.
7. The judgment to go flying, because as long as *he* doesn't have a reason to think he shouldn't fly then per the light-sport rules he (and every fully demented pilot can self-certify)…the paradox.
8. Now pay attention. Do you understand my snarkiness now? In the very rare instance when the NTSB bothers to get the necessary parts of a thorough accident investigation, we see graphic illustrations of how limited the toxicology report and autopsy are. This accident paints the picture of why the NTSB is tasked with the legal right to obtain medical records while also damning severely its focus on the appearance of the corpse's compound fracture injuries instead of on what medical factors might have played a role in the accident.

WPR13FA013

This was a strange accident. The pilot wrecked his airplane at about 5:00 a.m. in instrument weather conditions, per the NTSB. The accident is believed to have occurred about two minutes after takeoff, so a competent pilot would have known he was heading into IMC without any IFR certification and in an airplane that wasn't IFR qualified. Thus, clearly this pilot wasn't mentally competent, by definition.

We once again see the self-imposed limitations the NTSB places on itself, making a true accident investigation simply a farce. The seventy-five-year-old pilot was on a blood thinner. There aren't a lot of reasons for a seventy-five-year-old to be on warfarin. It almost always indicates a significant medical issue. Scratch that; the reasons to put a person on an anticlotting medication that requires regular monitoring by a physician is *always* a serious medical issue.

So here is what we know:

- A pilot with a blood thinner
- Seventy-five years of age
- Flying a light-sport aircraft at five in the morning in instrument conditions and wrecking within minutes of takeoff

What else does the report tell us?

A review of FAA airman records revealed that the 75-year-old-pilot held a sport pilot certificate with an endorsement for airplane single-engine land. The most recent FAA medical certificate was issued to the pilot in March 1985, with the limitation that he must wear corrective lenses for near and distant vision.

According to the FAA, the pilot was medically eligible to fly as a light sport pilot as long as he had a valid driver's license and was in compliance with 14 CFR 61.53 "Prohibition on operations during medical deficiency."

The pilot submitted his last medical application on March 7, 1985. He reported he had a total time of 157 hours with 28 hours logged in the last 6 months. According to FAA documentation, on January 17, 1992, the sport pilot voluntarily surrendered his Mechanic-Powerplant; Private Pilot-Single Engine Land and

Glider-Aero Tow; and Senior Parachute Rigger Certificates due to failing eye sight.

OK, now that is spectacular doublespeak. If he had failing eyesight and surrendered his other certificates, then he had reason to know he had a medical deficiency. There is zero evidence the NTSB checked to see if the gentleman had a valid driver's license.

Now listen to what the wife said: "When asked about the weather that morning, she recalls a light fog in the area."

It was 5:00 a.m. Night and fog.

This is the whole record of the investigators interview of the wife:

During a phone interview with Mrs. Hayden, she explained that she had dropped her husband off at the airport hangar where the airplane was stored the morning of the accident. Mrs. Hayden waited in the car while he pulled the airplane out of the hangar. As soon as the aircraft's engine started she waved, letting him know that she was going to relocate to the airport restaurant where she would see him off. She further stated as the aircraft taxied on its way to the runway she departed the airport to return home. When asked about the weather that morning, she recalls a light fog in the area.

Do you see what is missing?

There wasn't even a discussion of his eyesight or his warfarin use, or his underlying medical issues. He was seventy-five years old, took off in the dark in fog, and wrecked just off the runway. It is pretty clear why he wrecked. He lacked the judgment not to fly that morning. According to the NTSB's probable cause: "The non-instrument-rated pilot's decision to depart into instrument meteorological conditions, which resulted in spatial disorientation and a subsequent loss of airplane control."

This is classic incapacitation by mental faculty. The pilot was incapacitated mentally. Because of that incapacity, he chose for reasons that can only be described as demented to fly in conditions that were well beyond his ability. The paradox of the pilot who lacked mental skills to make good decisions is compounded by the paradox of the NTSB pretending to do an investigation while doing anything but a thorough assessment of the pilot it found to have made a bad decision.

CEN13FA078

This accident again demonstrates why you should dig into medical records. This sixty-nine-year-old pilot hit power lines while attempting to land. Toxicology reports prompted the NTSB medical branch to do what the NTSB medical branch should do anyway: get medical records.

The medical records were obtained because the tox screen showed the pilot was on a medication used in seizure disorders or in psychoses. The pilot was also taking three blood pressure medications and a diabetes medication.

What did the medical records show?

The personal medical records reveal diagnoses of hypertension, diabetes, high cholesterol, prostate cancer in remission, peripheral vascular disease, and bipolar disease with two psychiatric hospitalizations in the year preceding the crash. The records do not indicate that cardiac disease had been diagnosed.

Hopefully the carbamazepine was helping his bipolar disorder.

A lot of times the bipolar patient will stop medication and then become manic. When he or she wrecks a car or airplane during such times, toxicology is negative.

That is the point. The toxicology screen is just a piece—it isn't the integral linchpin of any good medical investigation.

How does a person with mania have any ability to self-certify? This guts the light-sport concept fully. The entire idea of a mentally ill person who self-certifies is one only a mentally ill person would consider sane. If you want aviation safety, you have to have oversight and objective evaluation.

ERA13FA227

This accident illustrates the value of the old adage: "All it takes for evil to triumph is the silence of good men."

This pilot had no business taking a passenger with him to the grave, and he had an associate who knew as much.

Here is the NTSB section that makes you realize that sometimes fellow pilots need to speak up or innocent lives are lost:

On May 4, 2013, about 1300 eastern daylight time, an experimental light sport S6S, N388KB, was substantially damaged when it impacted terrain during an uncontrolled descent near Suffolk Executive Airport (SFQ), Suffolk, Virginia. The private pilot and passenger were fatally injured. Visual meteorological conditions prevailed, and no flight plan was filed for the flight, which departed Williamsburg-Jamestown Airport (JGG), Williamsburg, Virginia, about 1230. The personal flight was conducted under the provisions of 14 Code of Federal Regulations Part 91.

According to an acquaintance of the pilot, who was also a light sport airplane flight instructor, he had known the pilot for several years preceding the accident, and had sold the pilot the kit from which he constructed the accident airplane. After the pilot completed construction of his airplane in 2008, the flight instructor flew with him several times. In flying the airplane, the pilot complained that the airplane was "too responsive" compared to the Cessna 172 he was accustomed to flying previously. The pilot subsequently flew the airplane seldom, though the flight instructor was not aware of what the pilot's specific currency level was.

About two weeks prior to the accident flight, the pilot advised the flight instructor that he would like to join him and the group of other pilots who planned to fly their similar make/model airplanes from their home base at Cambridge-Dorchester Airport (CGE), Cambridge, Maryland, to SFQ for the fly-in event held there annually. The flight instructor urged the pilot to perform some local currency flights prior to the trip, and offered dual instruction in order to practice takeoffs and landing; however, the pilot did not fly with the flight instructor between that time and the day of the accident. On the morning of the accident, the group of pilots delayed their departure due to the adverse weather conditions prevailing at SFQ. The flight instructor again suggested that he and the accident pilot take the opportunity to practice some takeoffs and landings while visual meteorological conditions prevailed at their home airport. The accident pilot again declined the offer.

The group, including the accident pilot, subsequently departed CGE, and after encountering deteriorating weather conditions, landed at Campbell Field (9VG), Weirwood, Virginia, to allow conditions to improve. After landing, the accident pilot advised the flight instructor that he had landed "hard." The pilot subsequently inspected the airplane, and after finding no damage, elected to continue the flight with the group.

The flight subsequently departed 9VG, and after again encountering adverse weather, the group diverted to JGG. A lineman at JGG recalled watching as the flight arrived at the airport. He described that following the first airplane in the group's successful landing, the accident airplane aborted its landing attempt and initiated a go around. The third and fourth airplanes of the group then landed without incident. The lineman described the accident airplane's second approach to the runway as "very erratic," and that the airplane was banking at an angle of about 30 degrees to the right and left and "porpoising" as it landed. Following the landing, the airplane taxied to the ramp where the lineman serviced each of the airplanes with fuel. The accident airplane's left fuel tank was subsequently "topped off" with 5.7 gallons of fuel.

The flight instructor described the wind conditions at JGG about the time of their arrival as "variable and gusty," and another pilot in the group described the wind as "challenging" and that it, "kept you busy." One of the other pilots in the group spoke with the accident pilot regarding his difficulty during the previous two landings. The accident pilot stated that he was having difficulty controlling the airplane with the passenger aboard and that the additional weight was, "throwing him off." After eating lunch, the group departed for SFQ.

An airport advisory service was operating at SFQ, and the three volunteers who staffed the service observed and interacted with the flight via radio as it approached the airport. According to the volunteers, the flight leader initially requested to perform a low pass down the active runway four. After completing the low pass, one of the airplanes landed on the runway, while the pilots of the remaining airplanes requested to land on an auxiliary turf runway. The first airplane landed uneventfully, but as the accident airplane approached the runway, it entered an aerodynamic stall during the turn from the base leg of the traffic pattern to the final leg of the traffic pattern. The airplane then appeared to recover from the stall and aborted the landing, while the last airplane landed uneventfully.

As the accident airplane approached the runway for a second time, it again appeared to stall during the base-to-final turn. The airplane again recovered from the stall, aborted the landing, and continued in the traffic pattern. During a third traffic pattern circuit, and while turning from the downwind leg to the base leg, the airplane appeared to stall and subsequently entered a spin. The volunteers lost sight of the airplane as it descended behind trees, and immediately began contacting emergency personnel and coordinating a response to the accident.

The passenger who died deserved better. We can already guess that this is an elderly pilot with no currency, no biannual, and on sedating medications. And I haven't even looked yet.

The pilot, age 73, held a private pilot certificate with a rating for airplane single engine land. The pilot's most recent FAA third-class medical certificate was issued on June 17, 2008, with the limitation, "Holder shall wear glasses which correct for near and distant vision while exercising the privileges of his airman certificate."

Review of the pilot's personal flight log showed flight hours logged between the time he began his initial flight training in 1991 and April 2012. During that period the pilot logged 231 total hours of flight experience. Of that time, 185 hours were logged flying almost exclusively Cessna 152, Cessna 172, and Grumman AA5B airplanes, all of which occurred between 1991 and 2002. The pilot subsequently logged 2.2 hours of dual instruction in the accident airplane make model in 2003, and 2.5 hours of dual instruction in 2008. Following the 2008 flight, a flight instructor endorsed the pilot's logbook for satisfactory completion of a flight review. No subsequent endorsements were contained within the log.

Beginning in October 2008, the pilot made numerous flights in the accident airplane after completing its construction. During the remainder of that year the pilot logged 9 total flight hours, all of which were in the accident airplane. In the subsequent years leading to the accident flight, the pilot logged the following flight hours annually: 2009, 18 hours; 2010, 0 hours; 2011, 14.5 hours; 2012, 13 hours. All of the hours logged were in the accident airplane, and included both solo and dual instruction received flight hours. The final log entry was dated April 29, 2012, and no subsequent flight hour entries were recorded.

And the toxicology report?

The FAA's Bioaeronautical Sciences Research Laboratory, Oklahoma City, Oklahoma, performed toxicological testing on the pilot. No carbon monoxide or ethanol were detected in the samples submitted. Unquantified amounts of Cetirizine and Metoprolol were detected in samples of the pilot's blood and urine. An unquantified amount of Naproxen, and 46.5 micrograms per milliliter of Salicylate were detected in samples of the pilot's urine.

Cetirizine can be sedating, and metoprolol can cause fatigue. What I would have liked to have is the pilot's last few years of medical records. Was the metoprolol for heart disease and the aspirin as well? Was there a history of atrial fibrillation? The gentleman was in his seventies; I'd love to see his medical records and his geriatrician's opinion of his mental status.

There is little question that a rational person wouldn't have taken a passenger flying with zero flight hours in the past year on a cross-country, while ignoring the advice of a far more experienced pilot, who had previously provided flight instruction. These are not decisions one would associate with sanity.

Additionally, it is pretty clear from this and several other accidents that the aviation community itself isn't adequately possessed of enough judgment to self-police and prevent such needless deaths. The passenger deserved to have someone take this pilot's keys away.

WPR13FA376

In this accident, a seventy-two-year-old pilot with multiple medical problems appears to have taken up flying as a seventy-year-old. He took himself and another person to their deaths when he lost control of the aircraft and was unable to pull the ballistic parachute because he had left in the locking pin. The NTSB investigator stated that the pilot's depression was well controlled with medication. The autopsy also indicated he had lymphoma and a brain tumor and had been complaining recently of fatigue, which is a symptom of lymphoma, brain tumor, depression, and other diseases as well.

How did the NTSB investigator determine the depression was well controlled? Well there are a couple of ways you could do this:

1. You could ask someone in the family, who will likely understand that lawsuits are potentially pending and will paint the pilot in the most positive light. Since that happens constantly, this makes the family member almost useless in the event of a pilot-caused accident.

2. You could obtain medical records, which are legal documents considered to be objective evidence. We all know that medical documents can contain mistakes, but the point is they are more objective and show a track record of patient care, as well as the equally important concept of patient compliance. They also disclose other issues, such as thoughts of suicide, other illness, and so on.

In this particular case, the medical office staff members of the NTSB did the second. They not only obtained medical records; they then spoke to the physician on the phone. Now, this is where it gets interesting. The objective legally binding medical records stated:

According to records from the pilot's primary provider encompassing visits from January 2005 until January 27, 2012; the pilot had a history of depression, fatigue, and treated skin cancer. The last note was dated June 10, 2013, two months before the accident. That note documented a history of low back pain secondary to a disc disease, anxiety treated with paroxetine ten mg daily, insomnia, migraine headaches, glaucoma treated with drops, and right foot neuropathy secondary to an ankle fracture.

The staff members also noted the following:

The NTSB Medical Officer contacted the sport pilot's primary care physician and in a phone conversation on February 12, 2015, learned that the pilot was in apparent good health during April 23 and June 10, 2013 visits.

According to the medical records, there were seven factors:

1. Glaucoma
2. Back pain
3. Right foot sensory deficit
4. Anxiety
5. Insomnia
6. Migraine headaches
7. And fatigue

Additionally, he had lymphoma and a brain lesion.

According to a phone call to the physician from a government official eighteen months later, "He looked good to me."

Do you see a disconnect with reality here? What do you think the physician is going to say when the medical records are already in the government offices and the patient is dead from an airplane crash? Besides that, even the best physician isn't going to have a clear view of a patient eighteen months after the patient died. That is the purpose of recording medical information. If we just used our memory, we'd still be bleeding people for things other than hemochromatosis.

So given what you know, would you fly with this pilot? This pilot had reason to know he shouldn't have been flying; he had multiple reasons not to take up a passenger. He did so anyway. He was not a thorough pilot, and he wasn't attentive to detail, either. The ballistic parachute pin that wasn't removed? It had a red streamer attached. Fatigue and depression can cause inattention to detail. The objective evidence suggests this person wasn't within control of the minimum mental faculties required for safe operation of aircraft. The autopsy, the pinned parachute, and the crumpled metal are pretty damning.

ERA13FA372

In this accident, a sixty-nine-year-old pilot and his passenger, a sixty-one-year-old pilot, took off into the air and almost immediately began a slow turning descent into the ground.

> A witness at the airport stated that he observed the airplane taking off from runway thirty, a 3,500-foot-long, 75-foot-wide, asphalt runway. The airplane accelerated and climbed normally to an altitude between 50 to 100 feet above the ground. The airplane then entered a slow right turn and began to descend until it impacted the ground and immediately became engulfed in fire. The witness added that he did not hear any engine anomalies during the accident sequence.

This sounds suspiciously like a medical issue.

This is the narrative report of the NTSB on the medical information.

> Autopsies were performed on both occupants by the Commonwealth of Massachusetts, Office of the Chief Medical Examiner, Boston, Massachusetts. The autopsy reports listed the cause of death for the pilot/owner as "blunt chest and abdominal trauma" and "smoke inhalation" for the pilot/ passenger.

Toxicological testing was performed on both occupants by the FAA Bioaeronautical Science Research Laboratory, Oklahoma City, Oklahoma.

So we are assuming the toxicology was negative? Well, let's look at the docket:

>> Amlodipine detected in Urine>> Amlodipine detected in Blood (Cavity)
>> Colchicine detected in Urine>> Colchicine detected in Blood (Cavity)
>> Metoprolol detected in Urine>> Metoprolol detected in Blood (Cavity)
>> Warfarin detected in Urine>> Warfarin detected in Blood (Cavity)

So we know that pilot had some type of medical issue requiring him to be on a blood thinner to prevent clotting. Clotting that could kill or incapacitate him. He died in a manner that suggests incapacitation. I think I'd like to see some medical records.

The passenger's toxicology screening was negative. But as we have beaten to death, this hardly rules out any psychiatric issues.

The witness interviews open up other avenues to explore medically:

I spoke with Ms. Pearson (previous owner of A/C) regarding the annual inspection and logs N83863. She informed me that she gave the logs to the new owner. They were in a pouch. She did not have an annual inspection completed but did hear after the A/C that an IA had refused to sign off the annual because the new owner was going to convert the A/C back to a 7AC model (it had been converted to 7DC some years prior). She told me the new owner mentioned to her that he had a heart condition and wanted to fly the C as an LSA so he did not need a medical.

A pilot who knew he had a heart condition, didn't want oversight, and felt that a heart condition shouldn't stop him from flying? Did he feel an annual was important? Yet, light sport rules are that you cannot fly if you have reason to know of a medical deficiency, and clearly this pilot did have reason to know of such deficiency, since that deficiency was the very reason he was choosing to illegally fly light sport (you can't legally fly light sport if you have reason to know of a medical deficiency that would be unsafe to fly with). This is so paradoxical that you'd have to be insane to miss the irony.

> I spoke with Mr. Thissell regarding the annual inspection of N83863. He informed me that he had not done the annual in a few years, maybe five years ago. He mentioned that his son was slated to perform the annual for the new owner; but once he learned that the new owner had plans to remove equipment to lighten the A/C so it could be flown as a LSA aircraft he declined to complete the annual. He has no knowledge who may have completed the annual inspection or if one was even accomplished. He mentioned to me that the new owner did not have a medical certificate and had no intentions of getting one.

The NTSB report has some other glaring omissions:

> According to FAA records, at the time of the accident, the airplane was eligible to be operated under the light sport aircraft (LSA) category. A local mechanic reported that the pilot/owner did not have a current medical certificate and planned to operate the airplane as an LSA.

There is no sign the aircraft underwent a fresh annual.

So what caused the crash and killed this gentleman with heart disease on blood thinner at age sixty-nine? The two pilots left the rudder gust lock in place. This is a good beginning for looking at medical issues that would make a person forgetful or negligent, things such as mental illness. No such investigation occurred.

All the evidence is that the aircraft hadn't had a fresh annual inspection for an extended period of time. Frequent inspections aren't a bad idea, for aircraft and for pilots. And if I am investigating an accident and I know that a 69year old is choosing to fly with a known cardiac condition, I am going to want to see if my employer, the US government, is also the gentleman's primary insurer and I will want to get this man's medical records, not demonstrate that I know he has medical issues but that I have no interest at all in obtaining them.

To recap: 1. The investigator stated an elderly man, likely with medicare, died in an airplane crash. 2. The investigator mentioned that the only reason the man was flying light sport was because the man knew he had a medical deficiency that would have made obtaining a third class medical certificate difficult. 3. Despite the extreme likelihood that the investigator's employer (the US government) was also the pilot's insurance company, the investigator didn't bother to obtain medical records.

CEN14LA192

When you read one part of an NTSB report, it is often easy to predict the outcome of the toxicology or the autopsy based on the not-so-subtle clues. This accident is one of those types.

Per the NTSB:

Federal Aviation Administration (FAA) records contained no record of the accident pilot ever applying for or being issued any pilot or medical certificates. In addition, there was no record of the accident pilot ever applying for or being issued a mechanic or repairman certificate.

An individual who shared a hangar with the accident pilot noted the accident pilot had been interested in "trikes" for years. The accident pilot reportedly did not have any "hands on" training; however, he was planning to obtain some flight training. A few days before the accident, the pilot was observed taxing the accident aircraft up and down the runway.

OK, so let's take a stab at the toxicology or medical information we'll soon be reading: bipolar disorder? Other mental illness? Amphetamine usage? Marijuana? Drugs? We are seeing a behavior that is predictive of a set of conditions.

Moving to the toxicology report:

An autopsy of the pilot was performed on April 10, 2014. The pilot's death was attributed to injuries sustained as a result of the accident. The autopsy report noted scarring of the heart muscle on the posterior left ventricular wall (myocardial scarring), mild coronary artery disease with 20 percent or less occlusion of the major arteries, and an enlarged heart (cardiomegaly). Microscopic examination related to the myocardial scarring did not reveal any evidence of acute or subacute inflammation.

The FAA Civil Aerospace Medical Institute forensic toxicology report stated:

No CARBON MONOXIDE detected in Blood;

No ETHANOL detected in Vitreous;

Cyclobenzaprine detected in Liver;

0.019 (ug/mL, ug/g) Cyclobenzaprine detected in Blood;

0.048 (ug/mL, ug/g) Dihydrocodeine detected in Urine;

Dihydrocodeine NOT detected in Blood;

0.223 (ug/ml, ug/g) Hydrocodone detected in Urine;

Hydrocodone NOT detected in Blood;

0.033 (ug/mL, ug/g) Hydromorphone detected in Urine;

Hydromorphone NOT detected in Blood;

Metoprolol detected in Liver;

Metoprolol detected in Blood;

Norcyclobenzaprine detected in Liver;

0.011 (ug/mL, ug/g) Norcyclobenzaprine detected in Blood.
Cyclobenzaprine is commonly used to treat muscle spasms.
Hydrocodone is a narcotic analgesic. Both medications can have
sedating effects. Metoprolol is commonly prescribed to treat
high blood pressure, angina, or heart arrhythmias.

OK, that was easy—narcotics.

What exactly happened during the accident?

On April 9, 2014, about 0830 central daylight time, an Aerotrike
Safari experimental light sport aircraft, N678TW, was substantially damaged when it impacted terrain after takeoff from runway
19 (4,021 feet by 60 feet, asphalt) at the Littlefield Taylor Brown
Municipal Airport (LIU), Littlefield, Texas. The pilot sustained
fatal injuries. The aircraft was registered to and operated by the
pilot under the provisions of 14 Code of Federal Regulations Part
91 as a personal flight. Day visual meteorological conditions prevailed for the flight, which was operated without a flight plan. The
local flight was originating at the time of the accident.

The LIU airport manager stated he found the aircraft about
0850 shortly after he had arrived at the airport that morning. He
did not observe any portion of the accident flight and was un-
certain of the exact time of the accident. There were no known
witnesses to the accident flight.

Let's do the same thing on the next accident. I'll tell you about the pilot's flying experience; you predict his medical issues.

WPR14FA165

The 80-year-old-pilot held a commercial pilot certificate with
ratings for airplane single-engine land, and instrument airplane

issued in 1972. His most recent Federal Aviation Administration (FAA) third-class medical certificate was issued in October 2007, with limitations that he possess glasses that correct for near vision. At the time of his last medical application, the pilot reported a total flight time of 1,800 hours.

An entry in the pilot's flight logbook dated June 22, 2013, indicated that he had received 0.6 hours of flight training with an instructor in a Cessna 152, practicing "maneuvers, stalls, slow flight"; however, the most recent documented flight review was completed in November 2007. According to the logbook, his total flight experience in the two year period preceding the accident was 15.1 hours. His total experience in the accident airplane was 3.1 hours, all of which occurred during 4 flights in the month leading up to the accident.

The toxicology report showed that he was on warfarin. This is significant because he was eighty years of age. There needs to be a good reason why a doctor would continue an eighty-year-old on warfarin. Besides that, there is a need for monitoring regularly, which would make finding the medical records fairly simple. This wasn't done. There simply was no interest in ascertaining what mental or physical issues this pilot had that caused him to improperly maintain his aircraft and to lack the judgment necessary to safely pilot it and to obtain recurrency training.

The probable cause was the partial loss of engine power due to an improperly maintained carburetor and the pilot's subsequent failure to maintain aircraft control.

So the NTSB report simply stated he was on warfarin for some unknown reason, and his autopsy showed he died from hitting the ground extremely hard. What else did the autopsy show? Nothing really significant. Some mild arteriosclerosis. His medical history would be really helpful to figure out what was going on with the warfarin and what other things were hiding in the closet.

What we do know is that he didn't fly very much, he didn't take good care of his airplane, and he wrecked because of it. One thing we always look at in a medical exam is general appearance. A slovenly appearance can be a fairly significant red flag. An eighty-year-old gentleman on warfarin is also a significant red flag. And again, we have a paradox. A pilot who isn't keeping up his own airplane asked to be the sole judge of whether he should be flying. To any outside observer, an outcomes-based assessment would likely have concluded he most definitely shouldn't be.

ERA15FA102

This was the last light-sport fatal accident listed on the NTSB website upon my finishing this search. It spells out, in full detail, the issues the NTSB has with not really attempting to discover what medical issues are at play when a pilot or passenger dies in a general-aviation accident.

In this accident, a pilot and his pilot-rated passenger attended an air show. They were witnessed revving the engine, and subsequently the aircraft nose lifted, and the airplane suffered a tail strike.

The narrative begins with a description of the crash:

According to local authorities, several eyewitnesses observed the airplane, during startup on the ramp, strike the tail of the aircraft on the concrete ramp area. A witness further reported that the pilot exited the airplane, walked to the back of the aircraft, returned to the cockpit, started the engine, and then taxied out for takeoff. No witnesses reported seeing the pilot look on the underside of the elevator or the tail of the airplane after the tail strike. According to a video taken by an eyewitness, the airplane was observed departing, climbing to about 300 feet above ground level (agl), performing a left turn, and then conducting a pass down the runway in the opposite direction. The video then shows the airplane performing a second pass, about 300 feet agl, down the length of the runway and then performing a left turn. The airplane was then observed continuing the left bank until the wings were nearly perpendicular to the ground, the nose of the airplane dropped, and the airplane was last seen in a nose down attitude descending behind the fuel tanks at the airport.

The toxicology report turned up a very low level of a sleeping aid. From there, the NTSB report dives into the aircraft, digging through it in great detail and comes up with the following.

Postaccident examination revealed that the elevator trim cable was separated from the trim tab.

Although it is possible the trim cable disconnected when the tail struck the ground during engine start (and would have been noticeable to the pilot if he had looked), the investigation could not conclusively determine when the trim cable separated or whether the separation contributed to the pilot's loss of airplane control. No other mechanical malfunctions or abnormalities were noted that would have precluded normal operation. It is likely that, during the low altitude flyby, the pilot inadvertently entered an aerodynamic stall while maneuvering and did not have sufficient altitude to recover.

The National Transportation Safety Board determines the probable cause(s) of this accident as follows:

The pilot's failure to maintain control while maneuvering at low altitude, which led to the airplane exceeding its critical angle-of-attack and experiencing an aerodynamic stall.

And there you have it.

Now, if you are reading this, you may be thinking, *What else does Shewmaker want? The toxicology wasn't remarkable—so what is the big deal here?*

Well, I'll answer that. When you do an Internet search of the pilot, you find out he had been on disability for years because of back issues. Does that have any impact on a pilot's ability to properly check a tail section, where he would have to bend over and look under the elevator? It just might.

Well, OK, but it would be really hard to get medical records, Dr. Shewmaker.

That might be, except that disability is usually a government-run program, and the number-one donor to the decedent's GoFundMe page for expenses was a medical facility. I am guessing his family physician knew him quite well, and I am also guessing it would be a snap for the US government to find out what the US government was paying him disability for. You just have to want to do your job, otherwise it is going to be obvious you didn't bother to try.

CONCLUSION

With that we conclude our review of the light-sport fatal accidents. What can I determine?

Seventy-five of these accidents I would clearly classify as medical accidents. There were a total of 142 such accidents listed on the NTSB website, using the timeframe of the light-sport-class rule, which originated 12 years ago, and the narrowed search of fatal accidents wherein a probable-cause report existed.

Thus, I can definitively tell you that at a minimum, 53 percent of all light-sport accidents were medically caused. A more likely figure is somewhere above 60 percent, since a lot of the cases I didn't classify as medically caused had elements strongly suggesting that a careful review of the records would have made them medical.

The important thing to focus on is that this is not a predictive study. It is not a sampling study. It is every single fatal light-sport accident we have access to explore. I can tell you that it isn't a statistical probability that most of these light-sport accidents were medically caused; I can tell you it is a fact.

This is powerful because most studies give you only a statistical probability of the results. In this examination, if you buy the classification protocol that I use, you have a 100 percent guarantee that more than

50 percent of the light-sport fatal accidents examined were medically caused. What does this all of this say about the NTSB? A closer look at this government agency helps answer that question. This is explored in chapter 17.

17

HEAD IN THE SAND

THE NTSB HAS a mandate from Congress. Under this mandate, it is required to investigate general-aviation accidents. It is supposed to determine issues found in accidents from which new ideas for aviation safety can be promulgated.

In a weird way, it has done this a little bit. By suggesting openly, by virtue of its (ahem) reports, that it has no idea how to properly manage accident investigations, the NTSB has helped highlight the need for some new ideas on how (commonsense) aviation accident investigations can be conducted.

First, let's look at the mandate and then explore the ramifications of a federal agency having the task of investigating fatal aviation accidents and the top levels of the organization blindly not realizing how openly they are displaying their lack of commitment to their assigned task.

The NTSB is tasked with investigating accidents in aviation and determining probable cause. It is then also tasked with presenting safety recommendations with a long view of improving general aviation, as well as protecting the public.

The aviation safety department of the NTSB is made up of 120-plus employees with a budget of $33 million. It is divided into geographic regions, and while it is tasked with investigating all general-aviation accidents, we have seen that the thoroughness of such investigations is demonstrably lacking. Further, we see this is a codified lack of thoroughness, which is systemic.

The reason there is a lack of thoroughness is at least fourfold: (1) an NTSB accident-investigation team more interested in and designed from the bottom up for major-accident investigations; (2) the focus on airframe and engineering as being items more worthy of fully investigating and understanding; (3) budgetary prioritization; (4) public interest in the singular accident event.

Let's take a look at the Federal Code of Regulations regarding the NTSB and accident investigations.

Codes 49 CFR 831.2, 831.4, 831.8, 831.9 all have tidbits of information that when we string them together state the following:

1. CFR 831.1 and 831.2 tell what the NTSB is responsible for: investigating US civil-aviation accidents and incidents.
2. The NTSB can delegate some investigations to FAA accident investigators. But the CFR still requires the NTSB be responsible for determining probable cause.
3. CFR 831.4 defines why the NTSB is tasked with this work: "to determine the facts, conditions, and circumstances relating to an accident or an incident and the probable causes thereof." These results are then used to ascertain measures that would best tend to prevent similar accidents or incidents in the future.
4. CFR 831.8 hints broadly at the significant flaw in the regulations: "the (investigator in charge) has the responsibility and authority to supervise and coordinate all resources and activities of all personnel, both board and non-board, involved in the on-site investigation." We have seen that this supervision, in fact, is lacking in the overwhelming majority of all accident investigations.

This provides the NTSB a natural methodology to shunt a lot of the investigative work to other personnel. In theory this can be a benefit. In reality the impression you quickly acquire is that it seems to have caused a certain lassitude among NTSB personnel in which closing an accident and moving on can be quickly accomplished in many cases, leaving the underlying causatives of the accident unconsidered.

But 831.9 is the real issue. It is the teeth of the wolf that the NTSB has chosen to be muzzled rather than unleashed. It gives the NTSB the power to fully investigate all human factors:

> Upon demand of an authorized representative...and presentation of credentials...any government agency, or person having control of...any pertinent records, or memoranda, including all files, hospital records, and correspondence then or thereafter existing, and kept or required to be kept, shall forthwith permit inspection, photographing, or copying thereof...for the purpose of investigating an accident or incident.

This, then, is a federal regulation authorizing the NTSB to obtain the readily and easily available records: Medicare, VA, hospital, autopsy, and so on.

Using this regulation and a computerized fax machine, obtaining all of these records would cost almost nothing. I could do it with petty cash in my home office if I had such an authorization.

As part of my practice, I gather records daily. It would be fairly simple for 120-plus NTSB aviation-safety employees to do the same. They do not do so in most cases. Sadder still is that this process could be easily automated so that a name, Social Security number, and date of birth could result in an instantaneous request for a swath of medical records.

We have seen the NTSB mandate. Let's explore what it actually thinks it should be doing.

One way to find this out is to look at what it describes as its process to Congress. This can be found in their yearly budget request. Using the 2016 budget request, we can glean the following information: "On Page 49 of the Fiscal Year 2016 Budget Request from the NTSB to the

Congress, the Aviation Safety Department is outlined. It was budgeted for 134 full time equivalent employees and 33,213,000 dollars."

Its mission is described as follows: "Investigate all air carrier, commuter, air taxi accidents; in-flight collisions; fatal and non-fatal GA accidents; and certain public aircraft accidents."

Interestingly, the words *incompletely, half-assed,* or *partially* are not included in this mission statement. Which would mean that the NTSB understands its mission isn't to incompletely investigate accidents, investigate half-assedly, or investigate partially, but to do so in a thorough manner.

There is an added bullet that states, "Investigate safety issues that extend beyond a single accident, to examine specific safety problems from a broader perspective."

This would indicate, then, that to extend your thoughts beyond a single accident, you would be careful to conduct proper and full investigations and discard any that are incomplete from use in further investigations, since a partial investigation would have biases within it that would prejudice any "broader perspective."

In other words, you would be better off studying ten accidents extremely thoroughly than half-assing one thousand. The biases and poor conclusions drawn from a thousand poorly investigated accidents would taint your conclusions, while the size of the data set would draw inaccurate assumptions from laypeople about your study's quality and scope.

Later in the budget, the agency describes the different types of accident investigations:

1. Major investigations—paraphrased: "a significant event...loss of life...considerable property damage...a new design...or significant public interest." In these instances, which are relatively rare, the NTSB launches a team of investigators.

2. Field investigations (public and private): these investigations are ones in which the NTSB usually sends an investigator to the

scene and a follow-up investigation is performed. Typically there is a fatality involved, per the NTSB.

3. Limited investigation: in this particular case, the NTSB doesn't always travel to the scene. An FAA inspector instead is the investigator on scene. The NTSB investigator often never goes to the site in these cases.

4. Data collection investigations: in these investigations, there is no serious injury and no public interest. A one-page report is completed.

5. Incident investigation: this is a broad field wherein "accident" doesn't fit the event, but safety issues may be raised that warrant a review. The budget report drops off a tidbit here: "When the NTSB conducts a full investigation of an incident, similar to an accident investigation, it determines probable cause."

This is an interesting sentence, because if you read it quickly, you miss what is implied. This sentence implies that probable cause is determined only during full accidents or incident investigations. In fact, the NTSB often issues a probable cause in incidents where it openly admits it hasn't investigated thoroughly. This may be an editorial oversight, but it misleads the public. Which isn't hard to do, after all; the public loves to cite NTSB information as fact when we have seen that the NTSB admits to Congress that not all investigations are thorough.

If you add the general aviation fatalities in the time period examined (2011–2013), you see that 1,390 aviation fatalities were reported to Congress. Of these fatalities, 123 were not general aviation. Thus, 91 percent of all aviation fatalities for which Congress authorizes $33 million for 134 persons to study occur under the heading of "general aviation."

One would presume that an organization that was serious about preventing accident fatalities and improving safety would want to reduce accidents by focusing on where the majority of accident fatalities occur: general aviation.

In the weeds of the budget document, we find the other reason the NTSB investigates some accidents utilizing a large number of investigators while others are given a one-page report: publicity.

This isn't conjecture on my part. We know the NTSB prioritizes publicity, because it mentions it explicitly in the budget request when describing which accidents get investigated.

The NTSB defines a major investigation as one that "typically involve[s] loss of life, multiple injuries, considerable property damage, new aircraft design, or significant public interest."

A data collection investigation lists one of its criteria: "Lack of high public or industry visibility."

The NTSB is saying it investigates based on publicity, and it isn't hiding from that. It is openly stating, "We care about the publicity of the accident far more than its relevance to improving the future of aviation safety."

The a priori limitations of using publicity as a reason for when to investigate thoroughly or not are a bit obvious. If you don't investigate the low-publicity accident, you are likely going to miss the reason you end up having a high-publicity accident. It is as if there is a mental disconnect wherein the NTSB isn't grasping that a more thorough investigation of low-publicity accidents might actually result in less high-publicity accidents.

It is hard to claim that your mandate is to look for the broad view toward eliminating future accidents if you really only show up when the cameras and the lights are on you. To be so brazen about your own career self-serving nature is something that one would find crass, were it not a Beltway normalcy. But I digress.

We don't actually need the NTSB to tell us that it cares about some accidents and doesn't care about others. We have seen it, graphically, in the actual cases wherein it has made a very conscious effort to be on the scene.

In the Cory Lidle case, wherein two people died and a professional baseball player was killed, we see in the NTSB narrative report (DCA07MA003) there are eleven NTSB staff members listed as participating in this relatively simple accident investigation. You can look at the last page of the NTSB narrative, and they are lined up, name after name. And I'll pretty much guarantee you that more than one bar conversation has since involved an NTSB "investigator" bragging about his role in this investigation, when the odds are fairly good he had never before or after been listed on a narrative report.

After all, a plane turning in a small space and hitting a building doesn't require eleven geniuses to figure out. So surely if four or five people died in the same airframe type, they would send at least an equal number of NTSB personnel?

Let's look at a couple of Cirrus accidents before and after the Lidle accident.

In the first accident, which killed four people (LAX07FA021) and which occurred just after the Lidle accident, six NTSB personnel were involved. Icing, ATC, pilot qualifications, and so on—all were part of the issues that required investigation. This investigation was far more important, in my opinion, to preventing future accidents as it addresses communications, cross-country decision making, clearance around re-stricted areas, IFR currency, competency, and preflight planning. Thus, if we wanted some lessons learned, more bang for our buck could be gotten out of this little old crash in the middle of Arizona than a crash into a Manhattan apartment. But I'm just spitballing here. The point is that there were twice as many people killed and twice as many nuances to this accident.

The fatal Cirrus accident just prior to the Lidle accident killed two people. It would appear that icing also played a major role in this acci-dent, and one NTSB employee was listed on the narrative report.

Publicity is a terrible reason to do an accident investigation. A quick search of the NTSB database shows that there are seventeen incidents/accidents and twenty-nine fatalities when you use Cirrus aircraft with a keyword search on "icing." Type in the keyword "apartment" and keep all other parameters the same; you have one listing, a pro ballplayer and his flight instructor flying into a building in unfamiliar surroundings.

The NTSB mission as outlined in the 49CFR831.4: "these results are then used to ascertain measures that would best tend to prevent similar accidents or incidents in the future."

It would seem to me that if *that* is the federal regulations and there is *no* mention in your congressional mandate about prioritizing fatal aviation accidents based on your being a sports fanatic or some other esoteric nonsense, that you would focus on the seventeen incidents and twenty-nine fatalities involving icing as part of your attempt to prevent future accidents, rather than on the singular instance of a plane hitting a building that happened to have a sports figure at the controls. But maybe that is just me.

What other parts of the puzzle explain the NTSB's fascination with avoiding real accident investigation?

Budgetary prioritization certainly is an understandable restraint on the activities of an investigating team. It shouldn't, however, prevent you from some very simple ideas that would cost essentially nothing and that you legally have a mandate in 49 CFR 831.9 to perform, collection of medical records. 831.9 is the part of the federal regulations that I find so baffling when I read NTSB accident reports.

Let us look once more at what this section of the federal regulations authorizes the NTSB to obtain: "upon demand of an authorized member of the board...any government agency or person [that is *any* person]...or any pertinent records...all files...hospital records."

In fact, in order to legally enforce such data collection, the next paragraph states, "The Safety Board may issue a subpoena, enforceable in Federal district court, to obtain testimony or other evidence."

In practical terms, the NTSB can easily obtain medical records simply by sending out a notice of subpoena to hospitals and doctors, and the vast majority of facilities wouldn't blink or fight at all. For almost zero true cost, you could obtain medical records on practically any pilot over age sixty-five or who utilizes the VA or Medicare without any difficulty. The records of pilots who didn't die on impact but were admitted into a hospital would also be easy to obtain and would often yield a treasure trove of other ancillary information that might influence a probable-cause finding.

Why doesn't the NTSB routinely work to get the medical records? You'll have to ask the NTSB that. Maybe there isn't enough publicity to make them realize that this question warrants an investigation. You can change that if enough of you ask. If enough of the public would ask the NTSB this question then this will be a high-publicity event, and we have seen that is the key to the NTSB's heart.

Snark aside, let's examine what the NTSB has to say about aviation accident causes on a percentage basis, using the NALL report, which is compiled by the AOPA "safety" branch, an ironic name, since I have never seen a parameter called "spreading incomplete or inaccurate information" in any safety manual.

According to the NALL report, in 2012 there was the following breakdown in mechanical versus nonmechanical accidents: 5 percent of fatal accidents in helicopters were mechanical, and 4.1 percent of non-commercial fixed-wing general fatal aviation accidents were mechanical; 56.8 percent of the accidents were single engine.

The NALL report also listed the phase of flight percentages where the fatal accidents occurred. Fuel management fatal accidents were 5.6 percent; weather 21.4 percent; takeoff/climb out 12.4 percent; maneuvering 17.5 percent; descent/approach 13.6 percent; landing 4.5 percent; other 24.8 percent.

People have used these percentages to misconstrue that these are the causes of the accident. In fact, these are the phases of flight when the accident occurred. This seems like a really dumb mistake to make, but here is how it has worked.

When you break down "other 24.8 percent," you find that in about 2 percent or less, the NTSB decides the pilot became suddenly incapacitated.

Illiterate people misconstrue this as 1–2 percent of accidents wherein the NTSB feels that the pilot was suddenly incapacitated to mean that Medical causes are only 1-2 percent of all crashes.

As ridiculous as that sounds, you hear this nonsense echoed repeatedly, clueless aviation "experts" writing that medical accidents are very rare, while missing that they didn't even read the NALL report with any basic level of understanding and that the NALL report never once makes the claim they pretend it is making.

Crashing during landing doesn't imply that the landing caused the crash. Yet that is the take-home message certain spokespeople pass along, which espouses such nonsense as "only 1–2 percent of accidents are caused by medical issues." They reach this conclusion because amazingly they seem to believe that being suddenly incapacitated is the sole and only way a person can ever be impaired.

And this false information spreads through the general-aviation community like a wildfire. It is swallowed as fact when, in fact, it is nonsense.

This false narrative ignores that a sedated pilot is rarely a good one to choose when landing your airplane. It ignores that a stoned or drunk pilot is also a bad choice. Yet, as we have seen, this is often what happened in the fatal accidents. The fact that the drunk guy died while landing doesn't make this a landing accident; it makes it a DUI.

The misuse of the NALL report language by writers purporting to have the slightest rudimentary concept of aviation safety would be hilarious, but people die. That puts a fog over the conversation. And speaking of fog, a person taking off from a socked-in airport is counted as a weather accident, even though the accident occurred when a pilot with no IFR rating demonstrated he or she lacked the mental capacity to make a rational go or no-go decision. Clearly this would be a medical accident, but it isn't counted as such by the NTSB. Thus, the people who don't bother to vet the NTSB simply regurgitate the cud they chew on and never truly fact-check.

The fact that the doublespeak and the misinterpretation of the NALL report begin within the very organization that publishes the NALL report is important for two reasons.

1. The AOPA has a vested interest in pushing an agenda: loosening pilot medical oversight. Hardly an increase in safety. So the publishing of a "safety report" by an organization dedicated to loosening safety standards is a head-scratcher.

2. This "safety report," which includes a section on "when accidents occur," has been perverted to turn the report into a tool that determines "when accidents are or are not medical." This fits into the AOPA's overall political narrative while being obviously false. It may not be intentional, but it conveniently fits the narrative while being completely inaccurate in its claims.

Why such doublespeak on the "safety expert's" part? It seems to be because they naively latch on to the concept of "sudden incapacitation" as being the sole and primary reason for a medically related crash. You would have to be certifiably insane to think that "sudden incapacitation" is the major concern in aviation medicine. And if it isn't naïveté, then it is simple dishonesty. This is a pure dichotomy. Ignorance or dishonesty. There are zero other options.

What I do know is that the AOPA isn't openly discussing that many of these accidents are medical. Yet this book and *Murder in a 172* show that this is the case.

The silliness becomes evident when you reflect that "sudden incapacitation" is just one type of incapacitation and hardly the sole causative of medical accidents. It is not even the most common medical cause in transportation accidents. The DOT doesn't think "sudden incapacitation" is the major issue in most automobile traffic accidents. They are far more concerned with gradual or partial incapacitation.

A person's judgment, clarity of thought, and rational thinking can cause impairments. Oxygenation plays a role in this; pain plays a role in this; medication and sleep play roles in this. These may not be considered "sudden incapacitation" events; these are, however, incapacitations. Certainly, the stoned pilot isn't "suddenly incapacitated" when he wrecks. He is, however, just as dead, and the accident was medically caused.

The definition of *incapacitate* is, "to deprive of ability, qualification, or strength; make incapable or unfit; disable."

Thus, a person can incapacitate herself through lack of qualification, ability, lassitude, injury, medication, disability, or judgment.

Total sudden incapacitation, however, seems to be the only form the "safety experts" realize exists when they focus on the narrative of doing away with pilot medical exams. And that is just silly.

This verbal assault on common sense is what drives the "safety experts" to wholly inadequate conclusions. It is almost as if they all need to be committed. Not to aviation safety but to an institution focusing on mental health.

We must get from a point where the NTSB pretends to investigate an accident in which the pilot has amphetamines, benzodiazepines, and marijuana in his system, while flying illegally, and the probable cause reports lists "cause of accident unknown" to a point where the NTSB has the integrity to say that when a person is on two highly addictive drugs with severe side effects either illegally or via prescription for two medical issues while flying without a license on marijuana that he died because his mental faculties were unstable.

The rest of the world reading these probable-cause and narrative reports can fully grasp that the NTSB is being cowardly and that accidents such as these are 100 percent medically caused. The only thing probable on the entire report is that the NTSB refuses to use the word *probable* appropriately. When is it ever in the NTSB's best interest to demonstrate without any defense that it is publishing reports that no sane person would find honest and forthright?

I believe the answer is simple. The NTSB doesn't think anyone is bothering to pick apart the nuances to see the sham it passes off as a report. I think it has learned over time that it isn't going to be closely called on anything as long as it isn't overly specific. Thus, it will avoid any real attempt to get to and present the truth. I also think, based on reading more than four hundred of these reports, that some ethical investigators realize this. They present the truth in the narrative report.

However, then, to protect themselves from the administrative overlords, they make the probable-cause report a vanilla farce of the truth. That is *my* probable-cause finding.

I also believe that it is plausible that in some rare cases the NTSB investigation moves past shoddiness into cover up and thus quite possibly becomes an act of federal criminal fraud on the part of the NTSB investigator.

If you ever had any thought the NTSB reports honestly attempt to obtain probable cause, please read *Murder in a 172*. Let's also revisit an earlier accident from the book you currently are reading.

WPR10LA104

Let us look at the decision tree any intelligent person would make. Let us designate all you readers the "accident investigator."

1. Is flying illegally a sign of a person with solid judgment? If yes, why?
2. Is smoking marijuana a sign of a person who has solid judgment? If yes, why?
   a. Escape from their daily troubles
   b. A pain syndrome
3. Are the amphetamines by prescription or by illegal actions?
   a. If legal, why? Weight loss? Attention deficit? And are they legal to fly with, according to the FAA?
   b. If illegal, is this person an addict, since he is taking an illegal, highly addictive drug?
4. Are the benzodiazepines taken legally or not?
   a. If yes: is it for insomnia, for anxiety, and are they legal to fly on according to the FAA?
5. Is there any sign in this pilot's actions that show any desire to follow laws?
6. Do amphetamines have a withdrawal syndrome?

7. Does Valium have a withdrawal syndrome?
8. Will symptoms recur if you stop the medications?
9. Since all three medications are available by prescription, did a request for pharmacy records make it to the major pharmacies in the twenty-mile radius from the pilot's home, or even the five-mile one?
10. Did it show the name of the prescriber?

So even though ten or fifteen more questions are also obviously needed, let's stop and consider:

1. If the pilot was taking these medications all via legal prescription, the absolute best-case scenario would be that he stopped these medications almost immediately after starting them and thus wasn't addicted and thus was having no withdrawal symptoms.
2. This means he stopped them right after telling a doctor that he really needed them for medical reasons that were debilitating to him. Thus, he flew with the medications in his system after not taking them long enough to develop withdrawal symptoms but at a level showing he had stopped the medication before flying enough so that they weren't impairing him. He wasn't having withdrawal, wasn't impaired by the drugs, and *was only suffering the major issues that required him to start the drugs, such as anxiety, attention deficit, and chronic pain.* Just those.

Based on the accident and the toxicology report, how does that "absolute best case" sound like it resulted in a pilot who wasn't impaired?

Meanwhile, don't forget, he was flying illegally and doing acrobatic-type maneuvers. What part of probable cause are we having difficulty with here?

It is almost as if the NTSB has hired an anti-publicity team to write its probable-cause conclusion. Here again is the excerpt:

Witnesses reported the pilot appeared to be performing aerobatic maneuvers and attempting to perform loops, as the airplane made numerous nose-high and nose-low maneuvers.
Estimates of the airplane's altitude varied between 300 and 500
feet above ground level. The witnesses stated that the airplane
was in level flight when the nose pointed down steeply 45–90 degrees, and then started to transition up. Just after the nose went
above the horizon, the right wing folded upward. The engine
then lost power and the airplane entered into a free fall. A post
accident examination of the wreckage revealed that the fracture
surface of the wing spar were consistent with overload forces being applied to the airframe. The pilot did not hold a pilot or
medical certificate. Post-mortem toxicology testing on the pilot
was consistent with use of methamphetamine, marijuana, and
diazepam, but there was no urine or blood available for testing;
therefore, it was not possible to estimate the last time when the
substances might have been used or whether the pilot may have
been impaired by that use. The operating limitations for the airplane noted that it was prohibited from aerobatic flight.

The National Transportation Safety Board determines the
probable cause(s) of this accident as follows:

The pilot's performance of prohibited aerobatic flight maneuvers that exceeded the structural limits of the airplane, resulting in an in-flight breakup.

I mean, if you really want to pretend a non-licensed pilot's marijuana,
amphetamines, and Valium were simply red herrings, uh, bent mirrors,
I have to ask: Why do I need to have NTSB investigating reports? Just
because Gomer Pyle isn't available doesn't mean you can't find someone
equally as skilled in basic human logic.

We would be better off having a group from a local sewing club or
book club figuring out the cause of accidents. After all, they would likely
not be so completely clueless to discount some of the six clues:

1. Illegal pilot
2. No medical
3. Drugs
4. Drugs
5. Drugs
6. Flying as if, oh, I don't know, he might have been impaired

I am not buying the overworked, underpaid argument on this one. The local pizza deliveryman working for tips knew this was an impaired pilot.

Here is the reality:

- You need a medical flowchart of record gathering and assessment of medical and mental faculties.
- You need to hire fewer engineers and more medical professionals.
- You need to split the accident into two parts: the engineering assessment and the mental/physical assessment.
- You need outside oversight to look into why this obvious step has been ignored.
- You need to interview NTSB personnel in depth and find out who has already made these salient points, because I would be extremely surprised if the shoddiness of these investigations isn't a result of upper-level management stratagems versus the investigators in the fields. No one with a brain would consider many of these accidents "cause unknown." The "cause unknown" has the stench of an upper-management decision fraudulently pushed onto the investigators.
- You need to clean house of any of these folks at the upper level who are found to have engaged in pressure on the investigators. I guarantee that the investigators with integrity aren't overly happy having their names attached to an edited and redacted mendacious report, after they went to the trouble to try to find the truth.

Additionally:

You need to make it a law that any accident involving injury that occurs has to have a toxicology report done at the same time that treatment has begun by the EMS. When the patient is found, blood vial for drugs out of arm and pain meds began on the other. This should be a commonsense decision. You can always discount the opiate in the system if other things are present and it is documented that treatment was already initiated. EMS doesn't typically give amphetamines or marijuana—or warfarin.

You need to ensure that the moment transport occurs, the patient's family member is contacted if possible and that the insurance carrier makes it onto the EMS form, as well as the primary-care doctor's name. You want this information before the family member remembers you are investigating a crime. The wife or husband or other family member should also always be asked to bring the pilot's meds to the hospital, even if the patient is DOA. Even if the spouse is savvy enough not to bring the narcotics and the nitroglycerin, the Viagra bottle will have the prescriber's name on it. You have to crack open Pandora's box and then know how to harness its information. You need to immediately work on getting the pilot's name, download his Facebook page or other social media, and, if possible and found, his place of employment.

In the event a pilot dies at the accident scene, the local sheriff needs to notify the next of kin, tell him or her that the pilot may have been in an airplane accident, ask the name of his doctor and his insurance, and then inform the next of kin the pilot has passed once it is verified the pilot is an actual family relation. This is a gentler way to tell a person that a tragedy has occurred, while ensuring you obtain the medical information before the family member realizes he or she needs to shut up. In some rare cases, this won't be possible.

In those cases, federal government requests for records should be faxed to common pharmacies and insurers.

The only thing the investigator would need to do in a computer/fax scenario is fill in the name once, and it auto-fills and sends.

Enter the SSN or the birth date into the auto-filled forms on the computer/fax and off goes the records requests. My suggestions don't add any time to the investigators' jobs yet. In fact, they likely save time, and the investigators probably wish this happened with their other forms.

What are those faxes I would propose be sent? They are requests for records to the following:

a. Medicare
b. VA
c. UnitedHealthcare
d. Blue Cross
e. Aetna
f. Humana
g. Cigna
h. Walgreens
i. CVS
j. Nearest hospital to the pilot's home, as well as nearest pharmacy

Alternatively, you could have a list of the major insurance carriers in the pilot's dropdown state of residence.

So now you have cast the net, which will generate the beginnings of a real investigation of medical causes, and the total cost to the US government is minimal because it can be computerized, codified, and auto-filled. Six weeks later you will have a response from all of them.

Let's say a gentleman has Medicare and uses CVS. The automatic fax retrieval would have eight "no records" and two records. These records would show everything billed on behalf of that pilot and all his medications. You are now in possession of his primary-care doctor and his medication usage and pattern of compliance. Now you get the treating physician's records. This is beyond helpful; this is the whole enchilada.

Now you go to the autopsy and the toxicology report. If they are negative for any drugs, you cross-reference to see if the patient was not taking medication he was supposed to be taking.

Then you also recheck the Facebook pages or other Internet info you gathered. You simply want to make sure you don't miss something, like a guy smoking a bong time-stamped one hour before he died. You have to make sure you don't miss the obvious. There are often clues to a patient's medical and psychological health listed on the pages of their social-media accounts.

Now, let us put this into a checklist form, starting with something along these lines:

Pilot deceased on site?

Yes. Blood immediately. Family immediately. Facebook and Internet search initiation immediately. Goals: freeze and collect any online information before anyone can destroy it. Obtain medical records immediately to prevent adulteration due to familial pressures or obfuscation.

If no:

Pilot transported by EMS?

Yes. Blood draws immediately during IV access and prior to opiates, documented by EMS. Search Internet pages. Send out records request to hospital and major carriers within state of pilot's residence or residences.

If no:

Pilot left on own then died without medical treatment or someone drove to hospital.

This would be a rare event. I am not sure I have seen a case, but it is a plausible if rare possibility, and I am fairly certain there have and will be such cases occasionally—for example, a plane down in a very rural area, and someone transports. You need hair-root samples; blood tests, although likely of little value; and an aggressive medical records search based on geographical radius from the pilot's home.

Now you send off the toxicology report, and you send a form to the medical examiner specifically asking for as full a medical history assessment as possible based on the corpse and other information they are able to obtain to find. Some of the medical examiners have been pretty much accident investigators, especially when compared with the "investigations" done by the feds.

Then you wait for the medical reports to come in. Does the insurance company list a primary-care doctor? Obtain records. Does the pharmacy indicate other physicians? Obtain records.

When you are done, paint a complete medical picture of Bob, the pilot. Include the pertinent details:

1. Did Bob give a crap about his health? (Did Bob frequently miss medical visits? Did med refills match his prescriptions?)
2. Was Bob morbidly obese? Complain of fatigue regularly? Was he noncompliant with diabetes?
3. Did Bob's wife tell you he was an awesome pilot while asking his doctor to pull him off the road?
4. You never say something ridiculous to demonstrate how fast you are willing to close the book on your make-believe fairy tale of an investigation: "The family didn't give us records, so investigation over." To use the wonky media-speak garbage that passes for investigative reporting these days, "It's bad optics."
5. One important part of the checklist: Did Bob lie on his last FAA medical exam? That immediately would make all his light-sport activity a crime, since you can only legally pass a flight exam if you are honest. The fact that you didn't get caught doesn't mean you were flying legally or that you passed the medical, only that you obtained one by fraud. This points to exactly why it is so important to get this information.

The NTSB has a nice little checklist for the causatives of about 4 to 10 percent of accidents. This allows it to look fairly aggressively at the mechanics of accidents as related to airframe and power plant.

Simultaneously, the pin-the-tail-on-the-donkey model for investigation of the 90 percent of accidents that are mostly medical or pilot error or training flaws simply isn't surviving in the light of day. If the NTSB wants to stop pretending to do accident investigations and actually not be laughed at for its ineptness, it needs to adopt as good and as valid a checklist for the 90 percent of accidents it currently seems to be studiously avoiding any real attempt at investigating.

It would be better if the NTSB investigated 10 percent of all accidents completely and totally than to farcically and erroneously publish completely flawed, inaccurate, and shoddy "probable-cause reports." At least then you could confidently do good scientific studies on NTSB accident reports. As it stands now, there is zero value to the NTSB accident database other than to point out a floor for the number of accidents that are medical and as a way to say what part of the road the car ran off. The foggy part, the landing part, the taking-off part—none of which tell you much at all about the cause of the accident. Until you have an actual database for making aviation safer, you create a safety hazard.

One suggestion would be to have a team that works the mechanics of an accident and focuses on the interface that traditionally exists between the FAA folks and the NTSB investigators. A second team could be an investigation team that comes up with all medical and personal causatives that could be related to the flight, since these are the causatives of 90 percent of accidents, and the medical factors for the most part are currently being whitewashed.

The medical team would rarely require travel. The work could be done via Internet gathering of information. This would save transportation and per diem costs while utilizing a medical investigation model that focuses on human factors, based on an aggressive and thorough understanding of a patient's medical biography. True probable causes would be assessed, after a six-month remediation course to teach the NTSB what the word *probable* means.

Other considerations are as follows:

- Autopsy interrogatory
  This would guide each medical examiner on what aviation specific issues to address
- Internet review
- Obituary review
- Hospitalization or transport, name of hospital/transport service
- All hospital records reviewed, labs that would indicate any liver, renal, other medical issue that isn't accident related

In short, do a thorough investigation.

There is one other lesson to absorb. When operated in VFR conditions, excluding all IFR and icing events, on an apples-to-apples basis with light-sport aircraft, the high-speed, high-performance Cirrus aircraft has a fatal-accident rate of under 1 percent of the entire duration of its service life.

Aviation done properly by healthy people can be a very safe endeavor. With proper oversight and real investigations, research, and results, we can foresee a time when a lot fewer passengers and persons on the ground are killed or maimed by pilots who are both lying to themselves about their competencies and being misled by the false narratives promulgated by various industry groups pretending to care about aviation safety.

It isn't enough to spout this information to you solely so that you can simply take my word for it. I would like you, the reader, to learn this information to the degree that you understand that these systemic issues result in a lack of thorough accident investigations, but also so that you understand the cynicism and/or naïveté of certain aviation "experts" who use NTSB reports as if they are sacrosanct and complete. The NTSB itself doesn't even purport them to be complete or thorough.

Further, I'd like you to be aware that dishonest bills put forth by extremely ill octogenarian senators solely for the purpose of revenge have no business making it through the Senate, yet, with donations to their cause from vested aviation "safety" groups (an ironic term if ever there was one), such bills have become law. I'd also like to remind legislators that the majority of people really against medical examinations of pilots are the pilots who are in the elderly age group and who are also strongly against going to the nursing home and giving up their car keys. The average voter would think it is insane to pretend the DMV licensing process is an appropriate determinant of a pilot's health. Hopefully, the true fatal accidents by the diseased pilots in this book make the point well.

The math is simple: there are sixteen thousand pilots in their seventies and four thousand in their eighties. Why the disparity? They didn't all turn eighty and magically give up aviation because they wanted to learn to scuba dive. Death and infirmity are real things, just like large X signs on runways that only a blind man would miss.

There are 329 million people in America whose only real concern in general aviation is that the US government does its job and does not allow a plane to land on the roof or attempt to buzz the schoolyard. These are statistics that the million people who care about aviation in America need to understand. Loosening medical standards that are already far too loose is not in anyone's best interests except the pilot who thinks he is Superman, drives like a snail, and thinks he is in the 1940s. Policy made solely to enable the demented to endanger the larger public is demented policy.

Until we have an NTSB actually dedicated to finding truth in accidents, we will continue to have dishonest cynical misuse of the NTSB findings by "aviation advocacy groups". Hopefully, you have read this book, and the NTSB reports listed, carefully, and you too now realize what a farce current US general aviation accident investigation has become.

ABOUT THE AUTHOR

JOHN A. SHEWMAKER, DO, is a senior aviation medical examiner. As a busy and passionate flight physician, Shewmaker speaks frequently to safety groups such as the Federal Aviation Administration Safety Teams and the Experimental Aircraft Association. Shewmaker is the author of *Murder in a 172* and *Flying under the Weather.*

Made in the USA
San Bernardino, CA
07 December 2016